This book belongs to:

....

Mrs Wordsmith®

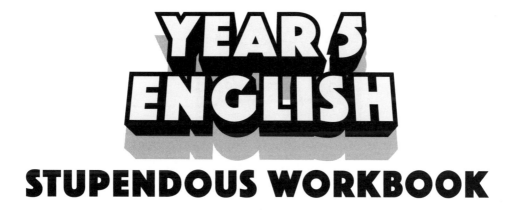

YEAR 5 ENGLISH
STUPENDOUS WORKBOOK

MEET THE
CHARACTERS

Yang

Bogart

Oz

Yin

Armie

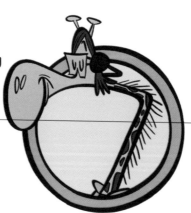

Shang
High

Bearnice

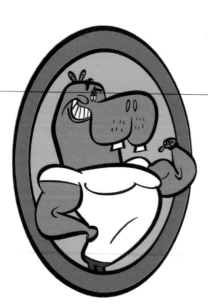

Brick

Grit

Plato

CONTENTS

Welcome to the Year 5 Stupendous Workbook!

What's inside?

In this book, you will find everything you need to gallop through English in Year 5. It is divided into five chapters: **Grammar**, **Punctuation**, **Vocabulary**, **Spelling** and **Reading and Writing**. Each chapter combines targeted teaching of key skills, illustrations and activities. It's perfect for those learning something for the first time and for those who are just revising!

How do I use it?

However you want to! Start in the middle, start at the end or you could even start at the beginning if you're feeling traditional. Take it slowly and do one section at a time, or charge through the pages like a mongoose on the loose! Don't worry if something is too difficult. You'll get there in the end and there are tips and reminders to help you along the way.

Look out for this icon at the beginning of a new topic. It tells you that there's some important learning to do before you start answering the questions!

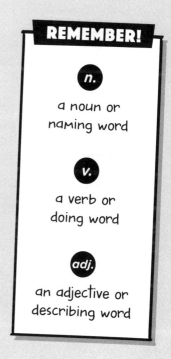

REMEMBER!

n.

a noun or naming word

v.

a verb or doing word

adj.

an adjective or describing word

How do I check my answers?

There's an answer key at the back! Checking answers is an important part of learning. Take care to notice and remember the ones you didn't know.

Oh, and please excuse Mrs Wordsmith's cast of out-of-control animals. They pop up all over the place and are usually up to no good.

Now, go and have some fun! And who knows, you might learn something along the way.

GRAMMAR

Grammar teaches you how to use different kinds of words (like verbs, nouns or adjectives) in all of their forms and to construct different kinds of sentences. When you master basic grammar rules, you have the power to talk or write about anything. When you master some more advanced grammar rules, you have the power to write beautifully.

A noun is the name of a **person** or **animal**, **place** or **thing**.

Proper nouns name specific people or animals, places or things. These always begin with a capital letter.

March   California   Bogart

Common nouns name general places or things. There are two types of common nouns: **concrete** and **abstract**.

Collective nouns name groups of people, animals or things.

Concrete nouns are physical things that you can see and touch.

Abstract nouns are things without a physical form, like a concept or idea.

family

crew

flock

window

magazine

noodles

safety

friendship

hatred

1 **Circle the abstract nouns and underline the concrete nouns in these sentences.**

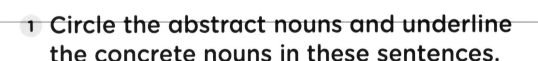

a. The bees are in danger.

b. He loves fashion.

c. The orchestra has incredible rhythm.

d. The truth was revealed at the end of the book.

e. The villagers all knew of her bravery.

f. Before the match, she is always full of excitement.

2 Draw lines to match the noun to its noun type.

proper noun	concrete noun	abstract noun	collective noun

swarm

ladybird

knowledge

rage

herd

Venezuela

dream

music

flag

December

flock

childhood

REMEMBER!

Some words, like "dream", can be either a noun or a verb. You have to look at a word's function in a sentence to be sure of its word class.

"I had a dream." – Here, dream is a noun.
"I dream all night." – Here, dream is a verb.

Verbs are **doing** and **being** words. A **doing word** describes an action (for example, **run** is a doing word).

A **being word** describes a state of being (for example, **am** is a being word).

You might remember that the way a verb is written changes based on whoever is doing the action or is in the state of being.

REMEMBER!

Whoever is doing the action or is in the state of being is also called the subject of the sentence.

When the subject is **singular**, add **-s** to the verb.

When the subject is **plural** or the subject is **I** or **you**, do **not add -s** to the verb.

He **shakes** his head.

They **shake** their heads.

1 Draw a line to match the subject to the verb.

These subjects can either be paired with **juggle** or **juggles** according to the rules above. Draw lines to match each pair.

I

we

Yin and Yang

she

they

Bearnice

juggle

juggles

2 Complete these sentences.

Circle the correct spelling.

a. Grit **grumbles** **grumble** when he's asked to do anything.

b. She usually **undertakes** **undertake** the most important job of every secret mission.

c. Bearnice and Bogart **gazes** **gaze** out over the horizon.

d. Yin and Yang only **solves** **solve** crimes on weekends.

e. You **hikes** **hike** to the top of tall mountains to see the spectacular view.

f. We **sneaks** **sneak** into the palace without being seen.

g. Shang High **rambles** **ramble** about music for forty-five minutes before he **realises** **realise** that no one is listening.

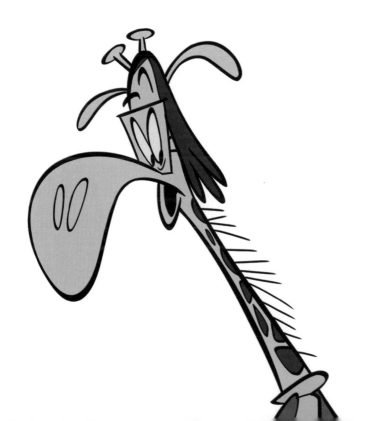

Modal verbs are used to change the meaning of other verbs.

The main modal verbs are **will**, **would**, **can**, **could**, **may**, **might**, **shall**, **should**, **ought** and **must**. These can express degrees of possibility as well as permission or obligation.

Brick **might** carry Bogart home.

Might is the modal verb here. It expresses the likelihood of Brick helping Bogart. It means that it is not certain that Brick will help Bogart, but there is a chance that he will.

Modal verb	How it's used	What it means
will (past tense: would)	She **will** dance later today.	It is certain that she will dance in the future.
can (past tense: could)	She **can** dance very well.	She has the ability to dance very well.
may (more formal than might)	She **may** dance later.	There is a chance she will dance in the future.
might (less formal than may)	She **might** dance later.	There is a chance she will dance in the future.
shall	She **shall** dance beautifully.	She intends to dance beautifully in the future.
should	She **should** dance now.	It is necessary for her to dance.
ought	She **ought** to dance now.	It is very necessary for her to dance.
must	She **must** dance now.	It is extremely necessary for her to dance.

1 Underline the modal verbs in these sentences.

a. Bogart may take over the world.

b. Shang High can make music.

c. Plato must open a new restaurant soon.

d. Armie will read one hundred books this year.

e. Yang ought to stop pranking people so often.

2 Read the sentences and answer the questions.

a. **Oz may read a book.**

Armie will read a book.

Who is more likely to read a book?

....

b. **Shang High must wash his socks.**

Yin ought to wash her socks.

For whom is it more necessary to wash their socks?

....

c. **Brick might play chess.**

Bearnice shall play chess.

Who is more likely to play chess?

....

Adjectives are words that describe **nouns**.
Let's look at some adjectives that are related to anger.

furious

adj. angry or enraged; how you feel when tickets for your favourite band sell out

WORD PAIRS

furious **reaction**
furious **pace**

resentful

adj. annoyed or bitter; how you feel when you think you have been treated unfairly

WORD PAIRS

resentful **sibling**
resentful **scowl**

irritated

adj. annoyed or peeved; how you feel when you fall into a patch of stinging nettles

WORD PAIRS

irritated **skin**
irritated **tone**

livid

adj. raging or furious;
how you feel when you
lose a video game

WORD PAIRS
---

livid **face**
livid **glare**

raging

adj. furious or
fuming; like an angry
bull on a rampage

WORD PAIRS
---

raging **bull**
raging **fire**

spiteful

adj. hateful or mean; like
purposefully spilling paint on
someone's work to ruin it

WORD PAIRS
---

spiteful **action**
spiteful **remark**

1 Complete these sentences.

Fill in the gaps with a suitable adjective that is related to anger. As these words have similar meanings, use the word pairs on pages 16–17 to help you.

| furious | resentful | irritated | livid | raging | spiteful |

a. "I already told you I don't want to come!" spat Oz in an .... tone.

b. Brick sprinted to the finish line at a .... pace.

c. The .... bull smashed the priceless vase without a second thought.

d. The losing team's captain shot a .... scowl at the referee.

e. Grit gave a .... glare to anyone who dared to talk to him.

f. Yang made some very .... remarks to Yin.

Adverbs describe **verbs**. Remember, a verb is a doing or being word.
Adverbs can often be made by adding -**ly** to adjectives:

furious + ly = **furiously**

1 **Complete these stories with the most suitable adverbs.**

As these adverbs have similar meanings, choose the one that best fits the context of the story, using the adjective definitions on pages 16–17 to help you.

irritatedly	**spitefully**	**resentfully**

a. Being twins, Yin and Yang share everything. This year,

Oz arrived at their joint birthday party with two gifts.

Yang instantly noticed that one gift was much larger

than the other. Yang stared ....

at her sister as Yin was handed the bigger present.

b. Drip. Drip. Drip. Grit tried desperately to relax. He sat down in a

comfortable chair and began listening to his favourite podcast.

Drip. Drip. Drip. The kitchen tap had been dripping all morning and

Grit couldn't seem to get away from the incessant noise. Drip. Drip.

Drip. Grit .... turned up the volume of his podcast.

c. Bogart had always felt misunderstood. After his fourteenth failed

attempt at world domination that month, he was feeling frustrated.

His friends, especially Armie, always got in the way of his genius plans.

So, Bogart decided to take revenge. He .... tore out

the last page of Armie's book. "He'll never find out how the story ends

now!" cackled Bogart.

Adverbs can also show how possible something is.

Some adverbs show it is **certain**
that something will happen.

Plato will **definitely** bake Oz a birthday cake.

Other adverbs show it is **uncertain** that something will happen.

Bearnice will **potentially** be late to dinner.
Brick can **probably** do a thousand push-ups.

1 **Are these adverbs certain or uncertain?**
Draw lines from the adverb to the suitable label.

certainly ◉

definitely ◉

maybe ◉

clearly ◉

obviously ◉

potentially ◉

perhaps ◉

probably ◉

possibly ◉

◉ certain

◉ uncertain

2 Rewrite these sentences and replace the underlined adverb with one that shows **more certainty**.

a. Bearnice <u>probably</u> forgot to tie her shoelaces this morning.

....

b. Armie will <u>possibly</u> finish reading the famous trilogy this afternoon.

....

c. The hissing snake was <u>potentially</u> very dangerous.

....

d. <u>Maybe</u>, Grit won't have a temper tantrum today.

....

3 Rewrite these sentences and replace the underlined adverb with one that shows **less certainty**.

a. Yang is <u>obviously</u> planning to prank Yin.

....

b. Shang High is <u>clearly</u> taller than all of his friends.

....

c. The cowboy is <u>definitely</u> going to ride into town tomorrow.

....

d. Forgetting your lines will <u>certainly</u> guarantee the play terrible reviews.

....

Adverbials describe how, when and where a verb happens. A **phrase** is a group of words without a verb. Some phrases behave like adverbs. These are called **adverbial phrases**.

Adverbials or adverbial phrases can be used to link ideas across paragraphs. This can be done using adverbials that express time, place or manner:

Time, for example, **earlier that day**

Place, for example, **on the moon**

Manner, for example, **in a terrible mood**

When these adverbials go at the start of a sentence, they are called **fronted adverbials**. Remember, fronted adverbials are always followed by a comma that separates them from the rest of the sentence.

1 Are these adverbials and adverbial phrases expressing **time, place** or **manner?**

Draw lines from the adverbials and adverbial phrases to the suitable label.

almost confidently

on the space shuttle

with a giggle

soon after that

as carefully as possible

a few minutes earlier

in the middle of the city

nearby in the bakery

time

place

manner

2 Read through this story and locate all the fronted adverbial phrases.

Underline the fronted adverbial phrases and say out loud if they express time, place or manner.

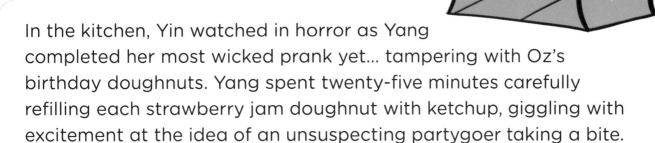

In the kitchen, Yin watched in horror as Yang completed her most wicked prank yet... tampering with Oz's birthday doughnuts. Yang spent twenty-five minutes carefully refilling each strawberry jam doughnut with ketchup, giggling with excitement at the idea of an unsuspecting partygoer taking a bite.

Four hours later, Oz's birthday party was in full swing. Brick was doing the robot on the dance floor, Bearnice was vigorously hitting a piñata and even Grit looked as though he was happy to be there. Very stealthily, Yang spied on the party through a crack in the kitchen door. She was feeling very pleased with herself.

3 Read through the rest of this story and add your own adverbial phrases in the gaps.

Oz called everyone into the kitchen ....

.... The guests all cheered and whooped when

Oz revealed a tray of delicious sweet treats.

"Why don't you have the first doughnut, Yang?" offered Yin. Yang

shrugged and reached for a custard doughnut, knowing they had

not been tampered with.

...., tears streamed down her

face as she tasted the spicy filling. "Mustard!!!" she cried. Everyone

erupted with laughter as Yin smiled apologetically at her sister.

Pronouns are short words that can take the place of nouns in a sentence. Without pronouns, sentences can get repetitive very quickly.

Subject pronouns replace the noun that acts as the subject (the noun performing the action) in the sentence.

Singular subject pronouns: **I you he she it they**
Plural subject pronouns: **we you they**

Bearnice gave Grit the ketchup.

She gave Grit the ketchup.

Object pronouns replace nouns that act as the object (the noun that the action is done to) in the sentence.

Singular object pronouns: **me you him her it them**
Plural object pronouns: **us you them**

Grit gave **Bearnice** the ketchup.

Grit gave **her** the ketchup.

Possessive pronouns replace nouns that show who owns something.

Singular possessive pronouns: **mine yours his hers its theirs**
Plural possessive pronouns: **ours yours theirs**

That bottle of ketchup is **Bearnice's**.

That bottle of ketchup is **hers**.

TIP!

The pronouns they, them and theirs can refer to more than one person, a person whose gender you don't know or a person who does not identify as male or female.

1 **Rewrite the sentence and replace the words in bold with either she or her.**

Use **she** when the words in bold are the subject (performing the action).
Use **her** when the words in bold are the object (having the action done to them).

a. **Bearnice** knows 436 facts about the ocean.

   ....

b. Yin chased **Yang** all afternoon.

   ....

c. Oz knew that **Oz** would win the dance contest.

   ....

d. The flying pie hit **Bearnice** in the face.

   ....

2 **Rewrite the sentence and replace the words in bold with either they or them.**

Use **they** when the words in bold are the subject (performing the action).
Use **them** when the words in bold are the object (having the action done to them).

a. Who pushed **Grit and Armie**?

   ....

b. **Yin and Yang** ran the marathon.

   ....

c. Please ignore **Bogart and Oz**.

   ....

d. **The twins** fight constantly.

   ....

e. **The two teammates** worked together.

   ....

3 **Cross out the words in bold and replace them with a suitable pronoun.**
Watch out, this activity mixes **subject**, **object** and **possessive** pronouns.
Use the function of the words in the sentence to help you choose.

his

Brick and ~~Brick's~~ treasure hunting team had been hunting treasure

successfully for years. **Brick and the team** worked together to follow

clues, decode treasure maps and break into high-security vaults.

They always shared the bounty equally. **Brick and the team** had

recently heard about a castle full of treasure at the top of a nearby

hill and nothing was going to stop **Brick and the team** from getting

their hands on it.

The castle was tall, grey and imposing. **The castle** was surrounded

by a moat with countless snarling crocodiles. Brick gulped. **Brick**

approached the castle door and fired an arrow directly into the

keyhole. Nothing happened. **Brick** fired another, but again nothing

happened. Brick and **Brick's** crew grew more and more frustrated,

hurling weapon after weapon at the door. **The door** didn't budge.

Suddenly, a small head poked out of the highest castle window.

It was Oz. ~~Oz~~ *She* didn't look happy. Brick saw **Oz's** face and lowered his bow and arrow.

"What on Earth do you think you're doing?" Oz shouted. "**I and the team** are here for the treasure!" Brick yelled back. Oz looked incredibly confused. "What treasure?" **Oz** asked.

Brick stopped. **Brick** looked up at Oz's castle and then looked around. On a nearby hill, **Brick** spotted a different castle, shimmering in the sunlight. **Brick** realised his mistake.

"Very sorry to bother you," Brick smiled at Oz sheepishly as **Brick** backed away from the castle. "It looks like we might have got the wrong address."

People speak in **complex sentences** all the time,
but when it comes to writing them down things can get tricky. When writing
complex sentences, there are certain things that you need to watch out for,
like when and how to use commas and whether or not to use certain
conjunctions (joining words).

A clause is a phrase that contains a verb. Complex sentences consist
of a **main clause** and a **subordinate clause**. The subordinate clause is
dependent on the main clause, meaning it does not make sense on its own.
It adds extra information to the sentence.

Here are three types of subordinate clauses that can make a complex
sentence: **adverbial clauses**, **relative clauses** and **non-finite clauses**.

Let's look at them one by one.

Subordinate clauses that begin with subordinate
conjunctions such as **because**, **after**, **when** or **until**
are **adverbial clauses**. This means that they add
information about how, when or where the action
in the main clause takes place.

main clause

Oz bought even more
popcorn **after the
movie finished**.

subordinating
conjunction

adverbial
subordinate clause

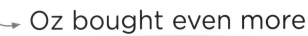

When an adverbial clause goes at the
beginning of a sentence, you need to put a
comma after it to separate it from the main clause:

adverbial subordinate clause

comma

subordinating
conjunction

After the movie finished,
Oz bought even more popcorn.

main clause

1 **Add the missing punctuation and circle the subordinating conjunctions.**

These complex sentences with adverbial clauses are missing punctuation. Add commas and full stops (where necessary) and then circle the subordinating conjunctions.

a. When nobody was looking the monkey grabbed a piece of fruit

b. When the laboratory exploded thousands of scientists lost their research

c. Grit had to walk to school until his bike was repaired

d. After picking apples all afternoon Plato made a delicious apple pie

e. Bearnice began to panic when she realised she was standing on quicksand

f. After getting new braces Oz's smile was brighter than ever

Subordinate clauses that begin with relative pronouns,
like **who** or **which**, are called **relative clauses**. Relative clauses
add information about the noun in the main clause.

comma

main clause → Armie felt bad for Bearnice, ↵

relative pronoun → **who had accidentally eaten
her pet goldfish**. ← *relative
subordinate clause*

When a relative clause with **who** or **which** goes at the end of a
sentence, it needs a comma before it and a full stop after. When it
goes in the middle of the sentence, it needs a comma before it and
another comma after it to separate it from the main clause:

relative pronoun   *relative subordinate clause*

comma
Bearnice, **who had accidentally eaten
her pet goldfish**, was feeling sad.

comma

1 Can you add the correct punctuation to these complex sentences with relative clauses?

Remember, if the relative clause is in the middle of the sentence, it needs
a comma before and after. If the relative clause is at the end of the sentence,
it needs a comma before it and a full stop after.

a. The bland food offended
Plato who was only
interested in bold flavours

b. The school which had
always been very traditional
started teaching
interpretative dance

c. Oz turned off the music
which nobody was listening
to anyway

d. Bearnice who had forgotten
to go shopping found some
pizza in the freezer

2 **Write a relative clause for these complex sentences.**

Fill in the gaps with additional information.

a. Brick, who ....

....

....

.... , stepped out into the blizzard.

b. The book, which ....

....

....

.... , was boring.

c. Bogart picked up the cookie, which ....

....

....

....

....

d. Bearnice stared at the painting,

which ....

....

....

....

....

....

....
....

Non-finite clauses often add extra information about the main clause by using a word that ends in **-ing**, like **seeing**, **running** or **being**. This type of clause is called a non-finite clause because it doesn't show whether the extra information happened in the past, present or future.

When a non-finite **-ing** clause goes at the beginning of a sentence, it needs a comma after it to separate it from the main clause.

When a non-finite **-ing** clause goes at the end of a sentence, it needs a comma before it. Unlike adverbial clauses, non-finite clauses have a comma separating them from the rest of the sentence, no matter whether they go at the beginning or end.

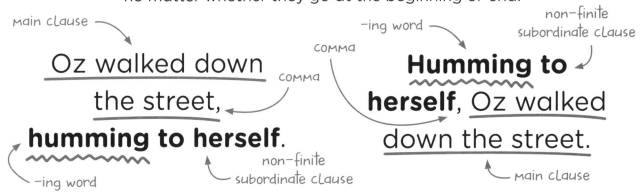

1 ## Complete the non-finite clauses in these sentences.

Choose the best **-ing** word below and fill in the blanks.
Don't forget to capitalise the first letter if the **-ing** word goes at the beginning of the sentence.

leaving   **getting**   **remembering**

a. Brick ran out of the door, ... his hat

behind AGAIN.

b. .... suddenly that it was

Plato's birthday, Bearnice picked up her phone.

c. Armie took another sip of hot chocolate,

.... frothy milk all over

his face.

Now that we've learned three types of complex sentences, let's practise using them!

1 **Rewrite these sentences so that the subordinate clause comes first.**
Remember to watch out for where the commas go.

a. Grit decided to start again after he added salt to the cupcake mix.

....

....

b. Yin thought she was more mature than Yang, being the older sister by

about ten seconds.

....

....

2 **Now it's your turn!**
Complete these complex sentences by adding a subordinate clause.
For an extra challenge, see if you can write an **adverbial clause**,
a **relative clause** and a **non-finite -ing clause**!

a. Bearnice climbed up into the treehouse ....

....

....

b. ....

....

.... Brick decided to go for a long run.

c. Bogart sent a letter to his aunt ....

....

....

Sentences can be formed in the **active** or the **passive** voice.
In the active voice, the subject of the sentence is doing the
action of the verb. In the passive voice, the subject of the sentence
is not doing anything. Instead, it is having something done to it.

active voice:

The subject
is doing the
action

**Grit watered
the plants.**

The subject is
having the action
done to it

passive voice:

**The plants were
watered by Grit.**

The subject is
having the action
done to it

**Yang climbed
the tree.**

The subject
is doing the
action

**The tree was
climbed by Yang.**

1 Rewrite the following in the passive voice.

a. Brick dropped the food.

....

....

....

b. Armie threw the litter.

....

....

....

c. Yang chased Yin.

....

....

....

d. Oz smelled the flower.

....

....

....

e. Plato's head blocked the screen.

....

....

....

2 Are these sentences written in the passive or active voice?

The passive voice does not always tell you who or what did the action.
You can say **The plants were watered by Grit** or you can just say
The plants were watered. Both of these sentences are passive.

Write **P** (for **passive**) or **A** (for **active**) above each sentence. If you get stuck, ask yourself whether the subject of the sentence is doing the action.

a.

Yang brushed her teeth.

b.

The window opened slowly.

c.

The dinner was prepared.

d.

The door was opened by the wind.

A preposition links a noun, pronoun or noun phrase
to some other word in the sentence.

Prepositions often tell us **where** (place) or **when** (time) something happens.
Examples of prepositions include words like **in**, **on** and **before**.

1 Circle the most suitable preposition.
Use the rest of the sentence as a clue.

a. The hot air balloon flew **over**   **during**   the city.

b. Armie brushed his teeth **before**   **besides**   breakfast.

c. Oz ran **to**   **until**   the train station.

d. Bearnice hid **between**   **under**   the table.

e. Brick played tennis **on**   **until**   dawn.

f. The astronauts landed **in**   **on**   Mars.

g. Yin and Yang napped **until**   **over**   3pm.

**2 Choose a suitable preposition
to complete the sentence.**

underneath   outside   during   until   on

a. It is Bearnice's birthday .... Friday.

b. Yin fell asleep .... the eight-hour movie marathon.

c. Shang High stood .... the music shop,

wishing he had enough money to buy the latest headphones.

d. Grit walked through the sewers .... the city.

e. Plato will close his restaurant .... tomorrow morning.

3 Fill in the gaps with suitable prepositions.

You should only use each preposition once so read through the whole story first to make sure you're using each one in the most suitable place.

over	beside	to	on	under	until

Bearnice travelled .... the centre of the desert, sweating profusely in the oppressive summer heat. After trundling .... hundreds of sand dunes, she stopped to drink her last few drops of water while sat .... a small boulder. As her hand rested on the rock, she felt a small symbol with the tips of her fingers. She gasped. This must be it.

Bearnice took out her spade and began to dig .... the boulder. She dug and dug .... sunset. Bearnice was about to give up when she heard her spade clang against metal. She knelt down .... her spade and peered at the metal. The rumours had been true. Bearnice had found the lost city of gold.

PUNCTUATION

When we talk, we use the tone of our voices to make our meaning clear. When we write, we rely on punctuation instead. In this chapter, you'll practise some key punctuation skills to help you make your writing more accurate and more expressive.

Apostrophes can be used to show contraction or possession.

Sometimes, apostrophes can show where letters are missing in shortened versions of words.

These shortened versions of words are called contractions.

REMEMBER!

Sometimes, the contraction does not exactly match the words that it is made from (for example, will not = won't).

You will love contractions.

You'll love contractions.

1 **Draw lines to match the words to their contractions.**

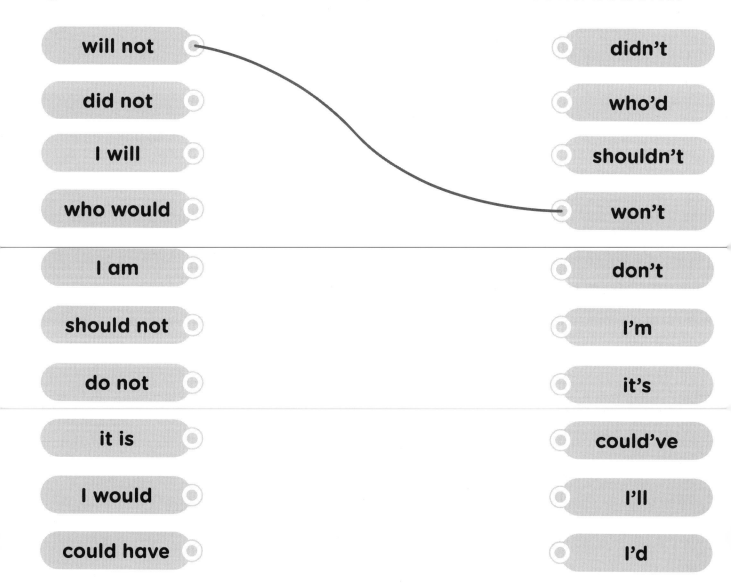

will not	didn't
did not	who'd
I will	shouldn't
who would	won't
I am	don't
should not	I'm
do not	it's
it is	could've
I would	I'll
could have	I'd

2 **Write the correct contraction above the words in bold.**

a. Once again, Bogart **did not** manage to take over the world.

b. Brick is the kind of person **who would** do anything for his friends.

c. "You **could have** warned me!" screamed Yang.

d. "**I would** be careful if I were you..." warned Grit.

e. **It is** a once in a lifetime opportunity!

f. Yang **should not** have sugar before bed.

g. Plato **will not** give up on his restaurant dreams.

h. "But... but... **I am** your sister!" cried Yin.

i. "**I will** never forget you," smiled Armie.

j. **Do not** touch the artwork.

3 Can you help fix the mistakes in bold?

Bogart is muddled! He wrote an **email to the owner of the Disguise Emporium**, but he wrote it in informal language when he should have written it in formal language.

Formal language is used when writing to people you don't know well or people you want to show respect to.

Edit the writing so this formal letter has no contractions.

Dear Owner of the Disguise Emporium,

I am
~~I'm~~ writing to complain about the quality of your disguises. Last

week, I purchased a giraffe costume. I definitely **didn't** buy this

costume as part of a plan to take over the world so please **don't**

ask any questions about that.

Your website claimed that **I'd** be unrecognisable in my disguise so I

confidently walked up to Bearnice and pretended to be our giraffe

friend, Shang High. Bearnice recognised me in seconds! **I'd** like a full

refund and **won't** be ordering from

your website again.

Yours angrily,

Bogart

4 Can you help fix the mistakes in bold?

Bogart is muddled, AGAIN! He wrote a **text to Shang High**, but he wrote it in formal language when he should have written it in informal language.

Informal language is used in more casual situations. It is often more friendly and more personal. Here, you can use contractions.

Edit the writing so the informal text has contractions.

Hey Shang High,

I am sorry I disguised myself as you. It was a silly idea and I **should not** have done it. I **did not** think Bearnice would realise it was me. I know it upset you, but I think **it is** quite flattering that I chose to disguise myself as you... I **could have** chosen anyone!

But **I will** pretend to be someone else instead next time. **Who would** you dress up as?

From,

Bogart

Apostrophes can be used to show contraction or possession.

You can show that something belongs to someone (or something) by using an **apostrophe** and an **-s**.

There are four rules about how you can do this.

1

You may remember that for most **singular nouns**, we add an **apostrophe** and an **-s**.

Bogart's plans are always villainous.

2

It's trickier when **singular nouns end in -s**. In these cases, we add an **apostrophe only**.

She copied **Charles'** homework.

He ate the **rhinoceros'** lunch.

3

When a noun has a **regular plural** (ending in **-s**), to show belonging, you add an **apostrophe only**.

The **cars'** windows were all smashed.

4

However, some **irregular plural nouns** (like one man, many men) do not end in **-s**. Here, you add an **apostrophe** and an **-s**.

The **men's** toilet is flooded.

1 Rewrite these sentences as phrases.

Use an apostrophe to show belonging.

a. The mansion belongs to Oz.

Oz's mansion

b. The diving equipment belongs to Bearnice.

c. The hat belongs to the octopus.

d. The magnifying glass belongs to the platypus.

e. The toys belong to the elves.

f. The kitchen belongs to the chefs.

2 Circle the correct word to complete the sentence.

It can be easy to get confused between **plurals** and **apostrophes** for **possession** because they often both end in an **-s**. Make sure you pay attention and only use an apostrophe if something belongs to someone.

a. There are lots of   cabbages   cabbage's   in the garden.

b. Those are the   bunnies   bunny's   carrots.

c. Where is the   teachers   teacher's   notebook?

d. The   spies   spy's   were on a secret mission.

Commas are there to help the reader. Knowing when to use them is important because if you use them too little (or too often!) it can make your writing difficult to understand. We're going to practise two ways that commas are used.

Commas are used to separate an introductory word like **yes**, **no** or **well** from the rest of a sentence, like **Yes, I would love some cake!** or **No, I haven't seen your motorbike.**

Commas are used to separate a person's name from the rest of a sentence when you are addressing that person directly, like **Grit, step away from the soup!**

When the introductory word or the person's name goes in the middle of the sentence, you need a comma before and after it, like **You know, Bearnice, your laugh is infectious!** When it goes at the end of the sentence, you need a comma before it and a full stop, exclamation mark or question mark after it, like **I don't think it's funny, no.**

1 **Fix these sentences.**
Add commas in the correct places.

a. "Your toast is ready Oz!" yelled Plato.

b. Yes I am aware that my shoes don't match.

c. Well I certainly wasn't expecting that.

d. No I will never stop making my own jam.

e. "Why don't you tell me about your day Armie?" asked Yin.

f. Tell me Bearnice do you have any bright pink rollerblades?

g. I am coming to the party yes but I still need to decide what to wear!

Commas are also used after **fronted adverbials**.

Adverbial phrases describe how, when or where a verb happens. When these adverbial phrases go at the start of a sentence, they are called **fronted adverbials**.

Fronted adverbials are always followed by a comma that separates them from the rest of the sentence.

FOR EXAMPLE:

At the bottom of the ocean, a slimy creature plotted his revenge.

1 **Correct these sentences by adding commas after the fronted adverbials.**

a. At 3 o'clock in the morning Plato clicked onto the next episode.

b. Twice a year Yang visits the crystal-clear lake.

c. Sometimes Shang High could be a little too prepared in an emergency.

Compound sentences have at least two main clauses
that are joined with a coordinating conjunction.

Shang High bought a new speaker **and** he listened to his favourite songs.

Coordinating conjunctions are joining words
that can connect clauses. Remember, clauses contain verbs.
The most common coordinating conjunctions are **and**, **or** and **but**.
They can be used to join two **main clauses** together.

Sometimes, adding a **comma** before **but** or **or** splits up the
sentence and makes it easier to read and understand.
Adding or not adding this type of comma is totally up to you!
This is called a stylistic choice.

FOR EXAMPLE:

Shang High bought a new speaker, **but** he dropped it almost immediately.

1 Tick the sentences that are punctuated correctly following the rules above.

Extra challenge! Correct the sentences that are not punctuated correctly.

a. Yin and Yang played football well but the opposing team won. ◯

b. Bearnice lost her socks but, her feet are not cold. ◯

c. Plato is an incredible chef, but he is a terrible dancer. ◯

d. Oz wants to learn German, or, she wants to learn Spanish. ◯

2 Turn these sentences into compound sentences.

Read the sentence out loud to decide which coordinating conjunction makes the most sense. Don't forget to add a **comma** before **but** or **or** if you think it'll make the sentence easier to read. It's totally up to you!

a. Oz might listen to classical music. She might listen to rock music.

b. She dreamed of changing the world. She just didn't know how to start.

c. It was a very humid day.

Bearnice did not mind at all.

d. Chess is a game for two players.

Bogart always plays alone.

Parentheses (singular: parenthesis) are words or phrases inserted as **extra information**, an **explanation** or an **afterthought** into a sentence that is grammatically correct without it. These are usually separated from the main sentence with two brackets, two dashes or two commas. First, we will focus on **commas**.

The painting, **worth £4 million,** was stolen late last night.

This sentence makes sense without the parenthesis.

This is extra information about the painting, but the sentence would still be complete without it.

Commas are used to separate parentheses when the writing is formal.

1 Add commas around the parentheses in these sentences.

a. Yang a notorious prankster snuck into the kitchen at midnight.

b. Armie sometimes called a bookworm reads fourteen books a week.

c. Shang High a giraffe who loves music knows every song ever written.

2 Rewrite these sentences and add the extra information.

Remember to add commas around the parentheses.

a. The bus driver never got lost.   **named Kai**

....

....

b. The thief logged into the bank system.   **a skilled hacker**

....

....

We have seen how commas can be used to separate parentheses from the main sentence. Next, we will focus on parentheses with **brackets**.

Bogart **(a cunning and nefarious fly)** is planning to take over the world.

This sentence makes sense without the parenthesis.

This is extra information about Bogart, but the sentence would still be complete without it.

Brackets are used to separate parentheses when you want the extra information to **stand out clearly**. Brackets are a better choice for separating your parentheses than commas when your sentence already uses a lot of commas. Too many commas in one sentence can make it messy and confusing!

Also, you can add **extra punctuation** within the bracketed parenthesis, like an exclamation mark.

Bogart **(a cunning and nefarious fly!)** is planning to take over the world.

TIP!

If the brackets go at the end of a sentence, the final punctuation mark goes after the second bracket. For example, "Bearnice high-fives Shang High (the tall giraffe)."

---

1 **Add brackets around the parentheses in these sentences.**

a. The house is haunted by three ghosts apparently from the 1800s.

b. Bogart surprisingly! didn't have a cunning plan.

2 **Rewrite this sentence and add the extra information.**

Remember to add brackets around the parenthesis.

The village was the first to be affected by climate change.

north of the mountains

....

....

We have seen how commas and brackets can be used to separate parentheses from the main sentence. Finally, we will focus on parentheses with **dashes**.

This sentence makes sense without the parenthesis.

My twin sister **— who is four minutes older than me —** really gets on my nerves.

This is extra information, but the sentence would still be complete without it.

Dashes can be used to separate parentheses when writing **informally** or when trying to emphasise a point in **narrative writing**.

1 Add dashes around the parentheses in these sentences.

a. Shang High a very tall giraffe needed special trousers for his long legs.

b. The chameleon a colour-changing lizard wandered through the desert.

c. Bearnice who had never had a driving lesson in her life sped down the motorway.

2 Rewrite these sentences and add the extra information.

Remember to add dashes around the parentheses.

a. Plato wandered into the kitchen.   **the hungry platypus**

....

....

b. A loud buzzing can be heard from the beehive.
similar to a vibrating phone

....

....

Writing with speech can be confusing because we often have a sentence within a sentence. Sometimes, it's helpful to think about the sentence as split into the **speech sentence** and the **real sentence**.

speech sentence

real sentence

"**Give that back!**" cried Yang.

The **speech sentence** always starts with a **capital letter** and sits between two **inverted commas**.

DID YOU KNOW?

Inverted commas are also known as speech marks.

Inverted commas go at the start and end of speech. There is always a punctuation mark before the final inverted comma.

If the speech sentence is a question, use a **question mark**.

"What's your name**?**" asked Bearnice.

If the speech sentence is an exclamation sentence, has a strong feeling or is said loudly, use an **exclamation mark**.

"She hates olives**!**" screamed Grit.

If the speech sentence is a statement and comes at the **start of the real sentence**, use a **comma**.

"Yes please," said Shang High.

If the speech sentence is a statement and comes at the **end of the real sentence**, use a **full stop**.

Shang High said, "Yes please."

When the **speech sentence comes at the end of the real sentence**, you need to add a **comma** before it. Remember, the speech sentence always starts with a capital letter.

Bearnice asked, "**W**hat's your name?"
Grit screamed, "**S**he hates olives!"

1 Fix these sentences by adding punctuation.

Add inverted commas and suitable punctuation marks.
Remember to add a comma before the speech if it comes second.

a. Where are we going asked Yin

b. Let go of my hair cried Bearnice

c. Plato announced I will never cook again

d. I'll do my best whispered Oz

e. Stop that thief shouted Grit

f. Oz asked Can I borrow the recipe

2 Rewrite the speech in the bubbles as full sentences.

Don't forget to use inverted commas and a punctuation mark before the final
inverted comma. Write at least one sentence where the speech comes second,
remembering to add a comma before the speech.

"Where is the gym?"
asked Bogart.

Paragraphs make your writing easier to read by grouping together ideas in sections. New paragraphs always start on a new line and, in narrative writing, can be used to group ideas according to **time**, **person** or **place**.

1 Add the paragraph breaks.

When we edit, we add // to show when a new paragraph should begin. Here is a fiction story in which four paragraphs have been squashed together. Read the text and decide where the new paragraphs should begin. The first one has been done for you so there are **two more paragraph breaks** for you to add in.

Shang High spent a lot of time by himself, not because he didn't have any friends (he actually had quite a lot of friends) but because he liked his own company. It gave him more time to focus on what he loved to do: make music and eat snacks. // One afternoon mid-jam session, Shang High heard a knock at the door. Begrudgingly, he took off his headphones and wandered towards the disturbance. He found a crisp pink envelope on his doormat. The letter inside read, "Tonight. 7pm. The castle on the hill. Wear your best suit." Oz had been secretly inviting all her friends to the party of the century. She had planned a twelve-course meal involving four different desserts, plenty of dancing, a bit of karaoke and maybe even a conga line. Everything had to be perfect. That night, Shang High arrived at the castle on the hill at 7:05pm. Fashionably late. He was dressed to impress in his best (and only) tuxedo. Part of him wished he was still at home in his comfy pyjamas practising guitar, but that feeling washed away when he saw the lavish decorations and glistening chandelier. Tonight was going to be a night to remember.

DID YOU KNOW?

To do something begrudgingly means to do it unwillingly, reluctantly or resentfully.

In non-fiction writing, paragraphs are often organised by topic.

A topic can be anything from tea to tractors to Timbuktu.

2 Which sentences could be in the same paragraph?

These sentences are all taken from a text about the **Amazon rainforest**.
Draw lines to match sentences that could be in the same paragraph.
Remember to read through all the options first.

a. Over 400 tribes live in the Amazon rainforest.

This fish has teeth on the roof of its mouth and its tongue.

b. The Amazon rainforest is found in South America.

The plants take in carbon dioxide (a greenhouse gas) and release oxygen.

c. The pirarucu is a meat-eating fish that can grow to nearly 3 metres long.

50 of these tribes have never had contact with the outside world.

d. The rainforest is vital for slowing down climate change.

He swam for up to 10 hours a day.

e. In 2007, a man swam the entire length of the Amazon River.

It spans across Brazil, Peru and many more countries.

Headings and subheadings are titles that tell the
reader about the text. They are usually found in non-fiction.
A **heading** tells the reader about the **main topic** of the text.

If the text is split up into smaller sections, these may have
subheadings to tell the reader what the **smaller section** is about.
Headings and subheadings can be single words, phrases or full sentences.

These different types of titles make the text clearer and easier to read.

1 ## Match the paragraph to the subheading.

The heading of these paragraphs is '**Butterflies**'.
Draw lines to label each paragraph with a suitable subheading.

BUTTERFLIES

Habitat

Size

Life Cycle

a.

Butterflies exist in
four stages: the
egg, the larva
(caterpillar), the
pupa (chrysalis)
and the adult
butterfly. Their
average lifespan is
two to four weeks,
but some butterflies
can live for up to
a year.

b.

They are found in
a variety of
different locations,
ranging from
forests to deserts
to grasslands.
Butterflies live
on every continent
except Antarctica.
This is because they
can live nearly
anywhere with
nectar-producing
flowers.

c.

Butterflies can
range in size from
1.3 centimetres
(western pygmy
blue butterfly) to
27.3 centimetres
(Queen Alexandra's
birdwing). They are
small creatures,
with the average
butterfly only
weighing around
50 grams.

2 **What subheadings would you give each of these paragraphs?**

These paragraphs are from a longer text called '**The World's Strangest Places**'. Write a suitable subheading for each one.

a.

....

This island off the coast of Brazil in the Atlantic Ocean has been called one of the world's deadliest islands. Ilha da Queimada Grande, also known as Snake Island, has the highest concentration of venomous snakes of anywhere else in the world. The snakes became trapped there when rising sea levels disconnected the island from the mainland.

b.

....

Uyuni Salt Flat in Bolivia is the world's largest salt flat. Salt flats are large, flat areas of ground covered with salt and other minerals. They usually shine white under the sun. The dreamlike expanse is visible from Incahuasi Island. Salt flats often have no vegetation growing but can have lots of wildlife. Uyuni Salt Flat is home to pink flamingos.

c.

....

The word 'forest' usually brings to mind images of trees and the colour green. The Stone Forest (or Shilin) located in China is distinctly grey. The huge limestone formations form a very unique natural scenery. Carved by wind, rain and earthquakes over millions of years, these rock formations are a natural wonder of the world.

VOCABULARY

Vocabulary is probably the most important part of learning to read and write. You wouldn't be able to read this sentence if you didn't know what all the words meant! The older you get and the more words you learn, the more you develop your word consciousness. Word consciousness refers to your awareness of the connections between words (like synonyms, antonyms and shades of meaning) as well as how words are built from various parts (like prefixes and suffixes or Greek and Latin roots). The deeper your word consciousness, the better you are at interpreting unfamiliar words when you come across them, which gives you the ability to read an endless supply of life-changing books whenever you want.

Prefixes are letters or groups of letters that are added
to the beginning of words to change their meaning.

The prefix **under-** means
under, **beneath** or **too little**.

under + achieve
= underachieve

meaning to do **less
well than expected**

The prefix **over-** means
over or **too much**.

over + sized
= oversized

meaning **bigger than
the usual size**

1 Transform these stories with the right prefix!

Pick the correct prefix and write the whole word in the gap to complete
the sentence. Say it out loud to make sure it makes sense.

a. Grit found a chest full of priceless

treasure while scuba diving

....

under   over water

b. Bearnice was meant to wake up

at 8am on Tuesday, but she

accidentally

.... and

woke up at 9am on Wednesday.

under   over slept

c. Yin and Yang struggled to travel through the

.... jungle.

under **over** grown

d. The midsummer sun was so scorching hot that it instantly

....

their eggs.

under **over** cooked

e. Grit spent all day cleaning up toxic waste in the

.... sewers.

under **over** ground

Prefixes are letters or groups of letters that are added
to the beginning of words to change their meaning.

The prefix **de-** means
opposite of or **not**.

de + hydrated
= dehydrated

meaning **not hydrated**

The prefix **pre-**
means **before**.

pre + fix
= prefix

meaning **the letters added
before a word**

1 Transform these stories with the right prefix!

Pick the correct prefix and write the whole word in the gap to complete
the sentence. Say it out loud to make sure it makes sense.

a. Grit looked at his

....

basketball and sighed.

(**de**) (**pre**) flated

b. Bearnice had to wait three hours

for her nose to

.... after

getting caught in the blizzard.

(**de**) (**pre**) frost

c. Grit gave everyone a

.... of his

latest (and greatest) song.

de **pre** view

d. Plato ....

a feast for the banquet, but Brick

ate it all while he was out.

de **pre** cooked

e. Grit's head hit the keyboard as

he dozed off. He was never going

to be able to

.... the

encrypted message.

de **pre** code

Prefixes are letters or groups of letters that are added
to the beginning of words to change their meaning.

The prefix **en-** means
to cause or **to put into**.

en + liven
= enliven

meaning **to cause to
be more lively**

The prefix **em-** is used instead of -**en**
when the root word starts with **b-** or **p-**.

em + power
= empower

meaning **to put someone in a
position of power**

① Transform these stories with the right prefix!

Pick the correct prefix and write the whole word in the gap to complete
the sentence. Say it out loud to make sure it makes sense.

a. Grit thought Oz had cheated.

Oz thought Grit had cheated.

Either way, they were both

....

(**en**) (**em**) **raged**

b. Yin wanted to celebrate her

victory, but she also

.... with

Yang's loss.

(**en**) (**em**) **pathised**

c. The motorway

.... the

whole forest, making it quite a

scenic drive.

en   **em**   **circled**

d. Bogart's bowling technique

....

everyone near him.

en   **em**   **dangered**

e. Oz's new sword-fighting skills

.... her to

go on a dangerous adventure.

en   **em**   **boldened**

Some nouns and adjectives can be turned into verbs by adding the suffixes **-ate**, **-ise** or **-ify**. You can use the original noun or adjective to give you clues about the meaning of the verb that has been created.

popular + ise = **popularise**
meaning **to make popular**

valid + ate = **validate**
meaning **to make valid**

person + ify = **personify**
meaning **to represent as a person**

Remember, when you add suffixes to words ending in **-e** or **-y**, you have to remove the last letter before adding the suffix, like so:

memory + ise = **memorise**

active + ate = **activate**

pure + ify = **purify**

Unfortunately, there are no rules about which words can be turned into verbs and which ones take **-ate**, **-ise** or **-ify**. You just have to know them! So let's practise.

1 Complete the table.

Write the words under the matching suffix.

alienate   simplify   solidify   equalise

modernise   standardise   captivate   advertise   intensify

diversify   notify   vaccinate   motivate

-ise	-ate	-ify

2 Fill in the blanks.

Choose the correct word for each sentence and add -**ise**,
-**ate** or -**ify** to turn it into a verb and complete the sentence.

| intense | captive | standard | motive | equal | modern |

a. Bearnice used unusual tactics to score a point and .... with the other team. Desperate times call for desperate measures.

b. "There's no 'i' in team, but there is an 'i' in 'win'!" shouted Brick to .... Grit.

c. Oz saw that a lot had been done to .... her old neighbourhood, but she missed some of the old shops.

d. The heat from the sun continued to .... over the course of the day.

e. Machines had been brought in to .... the production of teddy bears at the factory. Every single one was now exactly the same.

Some words are made up of different parts, such as **prefixes** (letters added to the beginning of a word), **suffixes** (letters added to the end of a word) and **roots**. The root is the main part of the word and carries the meaning.

Many root words, prefixes and suffixes in the English language originate from Greek and Latin. Understanding what these mean can help you work out the meaning of a word in English.

For example, the Greek root word **scope** means **see**.

micro**scope**

n. an instrument used for seeing very small things

tele**scope**

n. an instrument used for seeing things that are very far away

From now on, if you ever see a word with **scope**, you will know that it is probably related to the Greek root word and means something to do with **seeing**.

TIP!

When we notice things like root words, prefixes and suffixes, it helps develop our word consciousness. This is our awareness of words that helps us to spell and learn new vocabulary.

---

1 **Recognising different parts of a word is the perfect skill for a vocabulary detective.**

Let's get practising!

a. The Greek root **thermo** means heat.
The Greek root **metron** means measure.
What do you think **thermometer** means?

....

b. The Greek root **ophis** means snake.
The Greek root **phobia** means fear.
What do you think **ophidiophobia** means?

....

c. The Greek prefix **mis** means hate.
The Greek root **anthropos** means person.
What do you think **misanthropic** means?

....

d. The Latin prefix **ambi** means both.
The Latin root **dexter** means hand.
What do you think **ambidextrous** means?

....

2 Let's practise more!
Read the 'evidence' and draw your conclusion about
what each root word means.

a. A pseudonym is a fake name.
Pseudoscience is fake science.
What do you think **pseudo** means?

....

b. Fortitude is when a person shows strength during tough times.
A fortress is a strong building.
What do you think **fortis** means?

....

c. A microbe is a tiny organism.
A microscope is something that
you use to look at very small things.
What do you think **micro** means?

....

d. Demographics are statistical data relating to people in an area.
Democracy is a system of government where the people elect officials.
What do you think **demos** means?

....

Homophones are words that **sound the same** but are **spelled differently** and have **different meanings**. Near homophones are words that **sound similar** but are spelled differently and have different meanings.

This page introduces lots of different homophones and near homophones. Read through them and try to remember as many as you can because they will help you complete the next few activities. If you need some help later on, you can look back to this page for a reminder!

reek (v.) - After a few weeks the milk started to reek.

wreak (v.) - The giant monster wreaked havoc on the village.

stationary

stationery

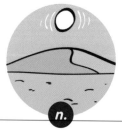

desert

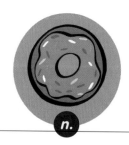

dessert

patients (n.) - The doctor really cared about her patients.

patience (n.) - You need a lot of patience to be friends with Yin and Yang.

led (v.) - The captain led her team to victory!

lead (n.) - Lead is a metal that melts easily.

jeans

genes

aloud

allowed

complement (*v.*) - Brick's new orange curtains really complement his orange wallpaper.

compliment (*v.*) - Plato refused to compliment Bogart's anchovy-flavoured ice cream.

advice (*n.*) - The agony aunt gave out terrible advice.

advise (*v.*) - I strongly advise you to take an umbrella!

guessed

guest

steel

steal

except (*prep.*) - There was nothing except a rotten apple in the fruit bowl.

accept (*v.*) - Please accept my apology!

effect (*n.*) - The hypnosis had no effect on him.

affect (*v.*) - The hurricane will affect many countries.

herd

heard

1 Fill in the blanks with the correct homophone.

jeans/genes   led/lead   wreak/reek   patients/patience   guessed/guest

a. Yin decided to .... havoc

at dinner.

Have a shower, Brick. You ....

b. Armie's .... was finally

rewarded when he caught an enormous fish.

They were the first .... to

recover from the mysterious illness.

c. Sometimes Yin couldn't believe she had the

same .... as Yang.

The perfect pair of .... can be

hard to find!

d. Plato .... the answers to most

of the questions.

Shang High hated hosting. He preferred to be

a ....

e. Oz .... Grit off a cliff.

The .... pipe must have been

used as a weapon!

steel/steal   allowed/aloud   desert/dessert   stationary/stationery   herd/heard

f. Brick trudged through the .... in the blistering heat.

Plato's wild idea was to serve

.... before the meal.

g. Oz found the perfect opportunity to

.... the wallet.

The triple backflip required nerves of

....

h. Plato blurted the answer .... and spoiled the game.

Bearnice .... herself to eat one more slice.

i. Yin and Yang wished they were

.... and on dry land again.

Armie kept his best .... in a personalised pencil case.

j. Oz's guitar could be .... for miles around.

A .... of elephants stampeded through the town.

2 Complete these sentences.

Fill in the gaps with the word **effect** or **affect**.

> **TIP!**
> Effect is a noun and affect is a verb.
> This can be quite tricky so think about what the word
> is doing in the sentence. Is it a verb or is it a noun?

a. Setting fire to my homework will definitely .... my

school report.

b. Plastic has a very harmful .... on the oceans.

c. This blizzard is certain to .... Plato's birthday plans.

d. Eating sweets can .... the health of your teeth!

e. The rainy weather doesn't really .... my mood

that much.

f. The sugary Halloween candy had an extreme .... on

Yin's energy levels.

3 Complete these sentences.

Fill in the gaps with the word **advice** or **advise**.

> **TIP!**
> Advice is a noun and advise is a verb.
> This can be quite tricky so think about what the word
> is doing in the sentence. Is it a verb or is it a noun?

a. Take my .... and buy some rollerblades!

b. Bearnice called to .... the president not to ban

dance-offs.

c. Oz realised she had given Grit some terrible ....

d. The official .... from the gym was not to wear shoes on

the trampolines.

e. I must .... extreme caution when walking the tightrope.

f. Shang High didn't know which .... to follow.

4 Complete these sentences.

Fill in the gaps with the word **except** or **accept**.

TIP!

Accept is a verb and except is either a preposition or a conjunction. This can get a little confusing so think about what the word is doing in the sentence. Is it a verb? If it is, then it must be accept.

a. "Please .... my sincerest apologies," said Bearnice to the snail she'd stepped on.

b. There is nothing in my attic .... piles and piles of completed sudokus.

c. Nobody knows about my secret hiding place .... my best friend.

d. Nobody would .... that Yang could jump the highest.

e. Brick likes all ice cream flavours .... pistachio.

f. "I .... defeat," said Oz on the verge of tears.

5 Complete these sentences.

Fill in the gaps with the word **compliment** or **complement**.

TIP!

There is a verb and noun form of both of these words, depending on how they're used in the sentence. To work out which word you should use, you have to think carefully about the meaning of each of them.

a. Bearnice wanted to .... Oz on her beautiful singing.

b. The actor knew how to take a ....

c. Armie and Brick make such a good team because they .... each other.

d. Oz has a different hairstyle to .... every outfit.

e. Armie hated flattery and never knew how to take a ....

f. The food critic offered a .... to the chef on his outstanding soufflé.

In the English language, there are many well-known **idioms**.
These are phrases or expressions that are used to share
a figurative meaning, rather than a literal meaning.

A **literal meaning** is when a phrase stays true to its actual meaning.
A **figurative meaning** is when a phrase means something more than
the most obvious interpretation.

The literal meaning of **two peas in a pod** is:

But the idiom **two peas in a pod** also has the
figurative meaning of **very similar, particularly in appearance**.
For example, **Yin and Yang are two peas in a pod!**

You may have heard of many of these and they can be used
to add style and character to writing! They can be used
to express complex ideas in a simple way.

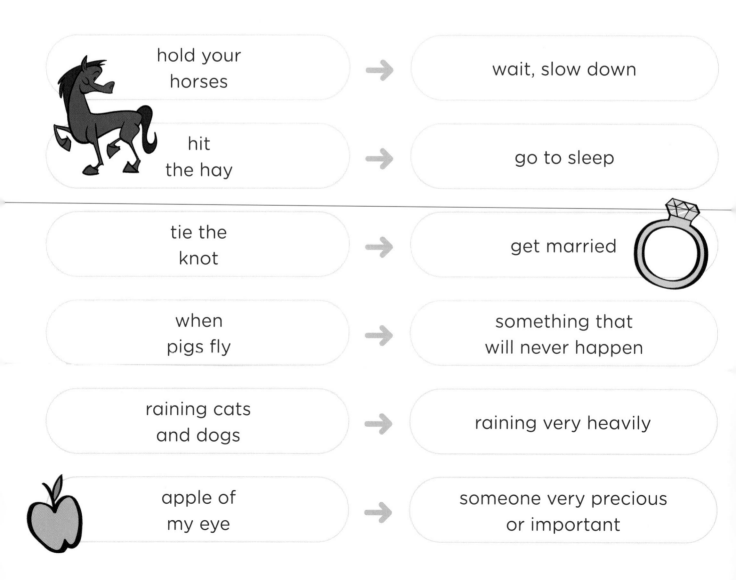

hold your horses	→	wait, slow down
hit the hay	→	go to sleep
tie the knot	→	get married
when pigs fly	→	something that will never happen
raining cats and dogs	→	raining very heavily
apple of my eye	→	someone very precious or important

1 Rewrite these sentences and replace the words in bold with an idiom.

Use the idioms on the opposite page or
any others you already know!

a. "It's time to **go to sleep**," announced Yin as she yawned loudly.

....

....

....

b. "**Wait**!" wheezed Oz as she struggled to catch up with Brick.

....

....

c. "I can't believe they're going to **get married** while skydiving!" cried Oz.

....

....

d. Yin and Yang had to cancel their afternoon plans. No one wanted to be outdoors while it was **raining this heavily**.

....

....

....

e. Bogart will **never** take over the world!

....

....

....

Vocabulary has the power to transform any piece of writing into something exciting. Take this simple sentence:

The superhero saved the cat from the tree.

By adding some adjectives and replacing a few of the words, the sentence is completely transformed. Now, it tells the reader a lot more about what happened:

The **fearless** superhero **leapt into the air and plucked the terrified** cat from the tree.

You need all kinds of words to tell stories. In this section, we'll learn some words to help you describe **water**, some words to describe **very difficult tasks** and some words that you can use instead of **sad** and **eat**. Repeating the same words all the time can get boring. Knowing these words will also help you with your reading because they are words you are likely to come across in books.

Next to each word you will find a list of **synonyms** and **word pairs** and an empty table with two columns. Sort each word in the list into the correct column.

A **synonym** is a word that means the same or nearly the same as another word.

Word pairs (or collocates) are words that are often found together in speech or in writing, like **fresh bread** or **fresh ideas**.

1

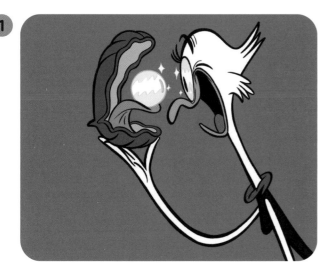

gleaming	water	beauty
sparkling	glistening	surface

word pairs	synonyms
water	gleaming

shimmering

adj. gleaming or glistening; like a precious pearl when it catches the light

Can you write a sentence using the word **shimmering**?

2

stale	swamp	still
foul	pond	air

word pairs	synonyms

stagnant

adj. stale or motionless; like a dirty, smelly pond where the water is completely still

Can you write a sentence using the word **stagnant**?

1

work	tiring	effort
exhausting	crushing	burden

word pairs	synonyms

backbreaking

adj. exhausting or crushing; like lifting something so heavy it hurts

Can you write a sentence using the word **backbreaking**?

2

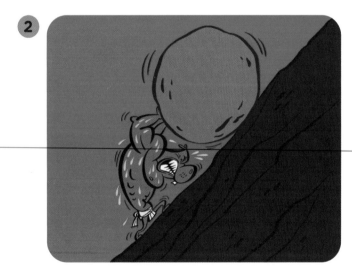

slow	undertaking	chore
process	exhausting	difficult

word pairs	synonyms

laborious

adj. difficult or exhausting; like the job of pushing big, heavy boulders up a hill

Can you write a sentence using the word **laborious**?

3

pressure	enormous	intense
urge	overpowering	weight

word pairs	synonyms

overwhelming

adj. overpowering or enormous;
like carrying a truckload of beach
equipment on your shoulders

Can you write a sentence using the word **overwhelming**?

4

dull	paperwork	process
boring	dreary	task

word pairs	synonyms

tedious

adj. boring or dull;
like having to work through an
endless pile of homework

Can you write a sentence using the word **tedious**?

1

silence	gloomy	mood
unhappy	expression	sad

word pairs	synonyms

glum

adj. sad or gloomy; when you feel like you're walking around under a dark cloud

Can you write a sentence using the word **glum**?

2

miserable	expression	tears
friend	inconsolable	crushed

word pairs	synonyms

heartbroken

adj. miserable or crushed; how you feel when all you can do is sob on the sofa all day

Can you write a sentence using the word **heartbroken**?

3

thoughts	sad	eyes
gloomy	sorrowful	song

word pairs	synonyms

melancholy

adj. sorrowful or gloomy;
like someone who feels sad
about everything

Can you write a sentence using the word **melancholy**?

4

longing	memory	sigh
sad	nostalgic	tear

word pairs	synonyms

wistful

adj. sad, longing or nostalgic;
like the sad feeling you get from
some memories

Can you write a sentence using the word **wistful**?

1

gobble up	a meal	a cake
a house	annihilate	destroy

word pairs	synonyms

demolish

v. to destroy or eat up; when you gobble something up until there's nothing left

Can you write a sentence using the word **demolish**?

2

a book	a sandwich	eat
gobble	consume	a meal

word pairs	synonyms

devour

v. to eat hungrily or gobble up; when you swallow your dinner in huge, hungry mouthfuls

Can you write a sentence using the word **devour**?

3

gorge

v. to stuff yourself or overeat; when you eat a giant mountain of food in one go and feel sick

| guzzle | stuff yourself | greedily |
| hungrily | shamelessly | overeat |

word pairs	synonyms

Can you write a sentence using the word **gorge**?

4

guzzle

v. to eat or drink hungrily; like gulping down a huge carton of milk all at once

| cola | devour | sweets |
| gulp | juice | drink |

word pairs	synonyms

Can you write a sentence using the word **guzzle**?

SPELLING

Using the correct spelling of a word helps your reader understand exactly what you mean. In this chapter, you'll master some challenging spelling rules, some spelling variations of common endings and some spelling patterns that come from ancient Greek and Latin.

When the **shun sound** comes at the end of a word, it can be spelled in different ways. Sometimes, the spelling of the root word can help us work out which spelling to use.

-tion   -sion   -ssion   -cian

1

Use **-tion** (the most common spelling of the shun sound) when the root word ends in **-t** or **-te**.

act → action

hesitate → hesitation

2

Use **-ssion** when the root word ends in **-ss** or **-mit**.

express → expression

permit → permission

3

Use **-sion** when the root word ends in **-d** or **-se**.

expand → expansion

tense → tension

4

Use **-cian** when the root word ends in **-c** or **-cs**.

music → musician

politics → politician

1 Circle the words that are spelled <u>incorrectly.</u>

injectsian   physician   magision   invention

discusion   permission   extension   confesscian

2 Write out the correct spellings of the incorrectly spelled words in activity 1.

....

....

3 Transform these root words into their form that ends in the **shun sound.**

a. mathematics ➔ ....

b. invent ➔ ....

c. electric ➔ ....

d. extend ➔ ....

e. operate ➔ ....

f. confess ➔ ....

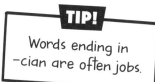

4 Complete these sentences using the words ending in the **shun sound** in activity 3.

a. "Maybe it's time to call an ....," admitted Brick as the lightbulbs exploded.

b. Shang High asked for an .... on his homework because he completely forgot to do it.

c. The surgeon has a very important .... this afternoon.

d. The lemon and lime drizzle cake was Plato's greatest .... so far.

e. Yang gave a heartfelt .... and admitted to everything.

f. Brick struggled to add two and two together. He was never going to be a brilliant ....

Sometimes, words ending in -**ant** and -**ent** sound the same
but are spelled differently.

brilliant   excellent

both endings are pronounced 'unt'

① Complete the table.

Underline the -**ant** and -**ent** endings in each word in the box.
Then, write the words next to the matching spelling pattern.

| innocent | instant | patient | hesitant | important | confident |
| distant | relevant | absent | frequent | tolerant | different |

-ant	-ent

② Add -**ant** or -**ent** to complete the words below.

a. dist..

b. toler..

c. inst..

d. frequ..

3 Read through this story.

Circle the words that are spelled correctly.

Grit had never been very good at being   **patiant**   **patient**   .

He paced back and forth, waiting for the news. Finally, he heard the

distant   **distent**   slam of a door. Bearnice was back.

Bearnice had been   **absant**   **absent**   all afternoon,

carrying out an   **important**   **importent**   and top-secret mission.

Grit's priceless painting had gone missing and he was convinced Bogart

had stolen it. Grit had asked Bearnice to sneak into Bogart's bedroom

and search for it. At first, she had been   **hesitant**   **hesitent**   .

It sounded like an awful lot of responsibility for one bear.

4 Read the second part of this story.

Fill in the blanks with some of the words ending in -**ant** and -**ent** from activity 1.

Grit rushed to the front door. He had been feeling ....

that Bearnice would find his painting until he saw the look on her face.

"I think Bogart is ....!" cried Bearnice. "Your painting

wasn't there!"

"So, there were no paintings at all?" demanded Grit.

"Well, there were lots of other, ... paintings in his

bedroom. They all looked important, but I didn't think those were

.... to this situation," admitted Bearnice. Grit sighed.

His suspicions had been accurate: Bogart was a thief. He just wasn't

the one Grit was looking for.

Sometimes, words ending in -**ance** and -**ence** can sound similar.
So can words ending in -**ancy** and -**ency**.

These words often have root words ending in -**ant** and -**ent**.

inst**ant** → inst**ance**   innoc**ent** → innoc**ence**

expect**ant** → expect**ancy**   frequ**ent** → frequ**ency**

1 Transform these words into their forms ending in -**ance** or -**ence**.

a. important → ....

d. relevant → ....

b. distant → ....

e. confident → ....

c. absent → ....

f. different → ....

2 Transform these words into their forms ending in -**ancy** or -**ency**.

a. expectant → ....

b. frequent → ....

3 Read through the story and circle the correct spellings.

Every year, Yin and Yang go on a salmon fishing trip. They have never been to the same place twice and no ⬭ distence ⬭ ⬭ distance ⬭ is too far! One year, they went to the Kola Peninsula in Russia, the next to Alaska in America and the year after that to the South Island of New Zealand. The twins planned to visit everywhere in the world that had an abundant supply of salmon.

The twins had a lot of **confidence** **confidance** in their fishing abilities, but they had some major **differences** **differances** in technique. Yin would sit still for hours on end, waiting for the perfect moment to reel in an unsuspecting salmon with her fishing rod. Yang would attack the water, swinging her claws frantically until she happened upon a fish by chance. Despite how wildly different their approaches were, they caught fish at roughly the same **frequency** **frequancy** .

4 **Read through the rest of the story and fill in the gaps with words from activity 1 and 2.**

These trips were usually uneventful, except for one fateful summer afternoon on a lake in Scotland. There had been a distinct

.... of salmon all day and the twins were starting to

feel hungry, and as a direct result, irritable. It was of the utmost

.... that they ate something soon.

Suddenly, Yin felt something tugging on her fishing rod. "I've got one!" she cried. Yin began to reel in the fish, but whatever was on the other end seemed to be much heavier and stronger than a salmon. A dark shadow approached the boat from deep under the water. Yin turned to Yang and, with .... in her voice, asked, "What do you think it is?"

"Don't panic," gulped Yang, "but I think it might be a shark."

Sometimes, words ending in -**able** and -**ible** can sound similar. These words are usually **adjectives**.

adorable   possible

Sometimes, words ending in -**ably** and -**ibly** can also sound similar. These words are usually **adverbs**.

adorably   possibly

DID YOU KNOW?

The suffixes –able and –ible usually mean "capable of being or doing something".

1 Complete the table.

Underline the -**able**, -**ible**, -**ably** and -**ibly** suffixes in each word in the box. Then, write the words under the matching spelling pattern.

considerably	possible
horrible	breakable
terribly	incredibly
adorably	dependable
incredible	comfortable
horribly	reliable
possibly	tolerably

-able	-ible	-ably	-ibly

2 Read through the story and add the -able, -ible, -ably or -ibly suffix to complete the words in bold.

Watch out for the word's function in the sentence to help you decide. If it is an adjective, it will end in -**able** or -**ible**. If it is an adverb, it will end in -**ably** or -**ibly**.

Bearnice loved getting her haircut! She saw it as an opportunity to reinvent herself every six months. Anything was **poss**..............!

She could go for shoulder-length hair, a short pixie cut or even

a Mohican if she felt like it. She always went to the same trusted and

reli.............. hair salon because they so often did an **incred**.............. job.

She sat in the **comfort**.............. salon chair and the hairdresser asked

her what style she was hoping for this time. "Surprise me!"

replied Bearnice.

The haircut was a **consider**.............. long process and the hairdresser

spent hours perfecting Bearnice's new look. Bearnice felt a bit nervous,

but she knew that the **depend**.............. salon would not let her down.

Four hours later, the stylist held up a mirror for Bearnice to see her new

hair. She gasped. The top was long with a dyed stripe of pink, the sides

were shaved and the back was bright orange. It was totally different

from any look Bearnice had gone for in the past.

For a moment the hairdresser thought she had done something

terr.............. wrong, until... "I love it!" cried Bearnice. "Thank you,

thank you, thank you!"

The /ee/ sound is most often spelled with **ee** or **ea**, but it can also be spelled **ie** or **ei**. Remembering whether the **i** or the **e** goes first can be difficult. Luckily, there's a helpful little rhyme you can use to help you:

i before e except after a soft c

So, in a word like **believe**, the **i** comes first. But in **receive**, because the /ee/ sound is after a soft **c**, the **e** comes first.

① Can you sort these words into the correct column?

These are all words that include an /ee/ sound spelled **ie** or **ei**.

| deceit | field | inconceivable | perceive |
| grief | ceiling | yield | niece |

ei	ie

② Write the missing letters in these words!

If you aren't sure, remember the rule.

a.

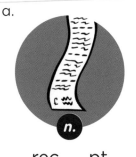

n.

rec......pt

b.

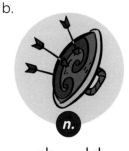

n.

sh......ld

c.

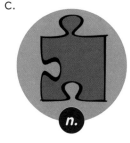

n.

p......ce

3 Circle the correct spelling of the words in bold.

Remember, **i** before **e** except after a soft **c**!

a. She calls her mum's sister **Auntie** **Auntei** Mia.

b. Would you like your **receipt** **reciept** ?

c. "Trick or treat!" **shrieked** **shreiked** Bearnice,

terrifying the neighbours.

d. Armie felt **relieved** **releived** when the thunder

and lightning finally stopped.

e. Bogart didn't always put enough effort into

his personal **hygiene** **hygeine** .

TIP!

Annoyingly, the "i before e except after a soft c" rule doesn't always work! It can be helpful a lot of the time, but you need to be aware of the exceptions, like protein, caffeine and seize.

There, **their** and **they're** are homophones, which means that they sound the same but they are spelled differently and have different meanings.

These words are very common and it's important to be able to spell them correctly, so let's get some practise.

There is used to refer to a place. You can use the question **Here or there?** to remind yourself of the spelling because **here** is in the word **there**.

I left it over there.

Their is a pronoun meaning **belonging to them**.

That is their TV.

They're is a contraction of **they are**. You can test if the word you want to write is a contraction by saying the same sentence with the expanded form. If it still makes sense, then it is written **they're**.

They're going to be five minutes late.

1 **Circle the correct spelling of there, their or they're.**

a. Armie and Oz put   there   their   they're   differences

aside in order to get the job done.

b. " There   Their   They're   never going to believe you,"

chuckled Bogart.

c. "Who put my slippers over   there   their   they're   ?"

demanded Grit.

d. Yin and Yang planned   there   their   they're   outfits

for the party.

e. Shang High never has any trouble with the neighbours

because   there   their   they're   never at home.

The letters **ough** can make many different sounds.
Some words that include **ough** are very common,
so let's get practising.

1 What sound does **ough** make in these words?

Here are lots of words that use the **ough** spelling.
Can you organise these words into columns, according to how they sound?

> although   bought   ought   plough   enough
>
> through   tough   brought   rough

words rhyming with "stuff"	words rhyming with "throw"	words rhyming with "short"	words rhyming with "blue"	words rhyming with "cow"

2 Fill in the blanks with the correct **ough** word.

Don't forget to add a capital letter if the word goes at the beginning of the sentence.

> rough   enough   although   ought   doughnut

a. Sandpaper is very ....

b. Bearnice ate a giant .... on her birthday.

c. .... she was tired, she couldn't sleep.

d. You .... to buy him a birthday card.

e. "There's never .... mayonnaise!"

snapped Plato.

Many root words in the English language originate from Greek and Latin. Sometimes, this origin can affect the pronunciation of a group of letters, for example:

Ch can be pronounced **/k/** like **chaos**.
Ph can be pronounced **/f/** like **photo**.
Sc can be pronounced **/s/** like **science**.

1 Complete the table.

Underline the **ch**, **ph** and **sc** spellings in each word in the box.
Then, write the words under the matching spelling pattern.

elephant	ache	chorus	physical	discipline
graph	scene	character	fascinated	scissors
alphabet	echo	descend	stomach	paragraph

ch	ph	sc

2 Fill in the blanks with words from activity 1.

a. It took a lot of .... effort, but Brick broke the world

weight-lifting record.

b. The explorer got absolutely soaked when the

.... sprayed water from its trunk.

c. It took all afternoon for the film director

to be happy with the fight ....

d. Climbing the mountain was the easy part.

Now they had to ....

3 **Read through the story and fill in the blanks with words from activity 1.**

Bogart's latest evil scheme to take over the world involved changing

the letters of the .... There would be no more C, no more

H and definitely no more Q. Of the twenty-six letters, only six would

remain in Bogart's new system: B, O, G, A, R and T. Children would only

learn those six letters at school. Every ....

of every page of every book would only use those letters (preferably

in that order). Every .... of every song would chant

"Bogart, Bogart, Bogart". His name would .... around

the whole word.

Bogart had run the numbers on this plan, calculating probability and

drawing up a .... to chart the data. It would take a lot of

hard work and .... to make it work, but it would be worth

it. He smirked, took out a pair of .... and started cutting

out pages from an alphabet workbook.

READING AND WRITING

Here, you will read character-rich fiction texts and illuminating non-fiction texts. You will answer some questions about the text and some questions that ask you to practise skills that you learned in the rest of the book. At the end of this section, there are prompts to help you take your writing to the next level.

In this section, we're going to focus on reading comprehension skills when reading non-fiction texts. Reading comprehension is all about reading a text carefully, taking your time and understanding it.

First, you're going to read a **news article** about **rising sea levels and the threat to the Pacific Islands**. Take your time and read the article slowly.

Then, use the text to help you answer the questions. If you aren't sure about an answer, go back and read the article again. All the information you need is in the text.

VOCABULARY

atoll

n. **a ring-shaped coral reef that can form islands**
The atoll is known for its circular shape and turquoise waters.

catastrophic

adj. **very damaging or disastrous**
The catastrophic thunderstorm left the whole city without electricity for days.

frontline

adj. **at the most important or affected part of a problem or disaster**
The city was very grateful to its brave, frontline firefighters.

precarious

adj. **likely to be harmed or in an insecure position**
The castle was in a precarious position, hanging off the side of the mountain.

injustice

n. **a lack of fairness**
She felt that a great injustice had been done and she vowed to put it right.

emissions

n. **the production and discharge of gases**
Emissions from the factory had tripled in the past three years.

Wordsmith Weekly

Vol. 237	22 OCTOBER	£3.00

RECENT REPORT SHOWS THE REALITY OF RISING SEA LEVELS

New findings by the Intergovernmental Panel on Climate Change (IPCC) show that within a century, entire countries may have disappeared entirely due to rising sea levels. This new research has alarmed scientists worldwide as it gives the international community much less time to address climate change and to reverse these trends than was previously thought.

According to the National Aeronautics and Space Administration (NASA), seas are rising by about 3.3 millimetres every year. While this number may not sound huge, the differences such increases make are monumental.

Rising sea levels are a direct result of climate change. There are two factors that cause sea levels to rise. The melting of ice in polar regions means that there is more water than ever in the oceans and the heating of the oceans themselves causes water to expand and take up more space.

Low-lying islands and atolls in the Pacific Ocean, where frontline communities live, are especially at risk. In fact, rising global temperatures have not only resulted in the shrinking of these islands, they have also increased the number of catastrophic weather events, such as droughts and devastating storms, that occur in these places. The IPCC report shows just how vulnerable some communities are to these changing conditions.

The Pacific Islands have provided people with a sheltered place to live for thousands of years, but now life on the islands is becoming increasingly precarious. Many have pointed out the injustice in this.

Pacific Island countries are some of the lowest carbon-emitting countries in the world and yet they are also some of the most at risk from the effects of global warming that are caused by carbon emissions.

For people living in Pacific Island nations like Tuvalu or the Marshall Islands, shrinking land and increasingly extreme weather conditions have been a part of life for some time now. It is yet to be seen whether reports such as the one published by the IPCC will raise enough awareness worldwide to force larger and more economically developed countries to take action.

1 **Which of these sentences best describes the reality of rising sea levels that is referred to in the headline?**

Put a tick next to the sentence that best answers the question.

a. Sea levels are rising most slowly in the Pacific Ocean. ◯

b. Rising sea levels threaten everyone, equally. ◯

c. Sea levels are rising faster than previously thought. ◯

2 **What does IPCC stand for?**

....

....

3 Find and circle the modal verb
in the first paragraph of the article.
What does this modal verb tell us about the author's intended meaning?
Put a tick next to the correct answer.

a. It is certain that
countries will have
disappeared within
a century.

b. It is not likely that
countries will have
disappeared within
a century.

c. It is possible that
countries will have
disappeared within
a century.

4 Find and copy one factor that causes sea levels to rise.

....

....

5 Based on the information in the article, why do
you think low-lying countries are at a greater risk?

....

....

....

6 Who does the author of the article think
is most to blame for the rising sea levels?
Circle the correct answer.

Tuvalu

more economically
developed countries

NASA

7 What is the **injustice** mentioned in the article?
Explain in your own words.

....

....

First, you're going to read an **explanation text** about **wind power**.
Take your time and read the text slowly.

Then, use the text to help you answer the questions.
If you aren't sure about an answer, go back and read the article again.
All the information you need is in the text

DID YOU KNOW?

Explanation texts help you understand how things work.

VOCABULARY

Before you read the explanation text,
here are some key words to help you.

agriculture

n. **the science or practice of farming**
The farmer had been working in agriculture all her life.

kinetic energy

n. **the energy an object has due to its movement**
When you throw a ball, the movement gives the ball kinetic energy.

finite

adj. **limited in size or amount**
The funding for the theme park was finite so only half the roller coasters could be built.

temperamental

adj. **unpredictable in behaviour, mood or performance**
It was hard to predict how the temperamental professor would react.

WIND POWER

Renewable energy is energy generated from a source that is not lessened when used. It includes power from oceans, the Sun and wind. These sources of energy are popular amongst the environmentally conscious because they do not use up the Earth's finite resources to produce electricity and release no (or substantially less) harmful gas.

Windmills

Wind power has been popular on a small scale for centuries. The first windmills were built around the 9th century in the Middle East and Asia to use wind power for agricultural tasks, such as grinding grain and pumping water. Wind would spin the blades of the windmill, rotating the centre shaft. This in turn would spin a grain mill, which are large, flat stones, to grind grain and produce flour. The rotation of the centre shaft could also be used to drive a water pump, providing water to nearby houses.

Wind Turbines

Wind power is still used in a similar way to this day, but instead of converting the spinning energy into mechanical work (like grinding grain and pumping water) it is converted into electricity. These devices are called wind turbines. They are believed to have been invented in 1887 by Professor James Blyth in Glasgow, Scotland.

Wind Farms

Wind farms are a collection of wind turbines in the same area used to generate electricity. To do this, the farms are built in flat, open areas where the wind blows consistently, ideally at a minimum of 10 miles per hour. The number of wind turbines on a farm can vary dramatically. The Jiuquan Wind Power Base in China is the largest wind farm in the world, with a planned installation of 7,000 wind turbines.

How Wind Turbines Work

To be near the stronger air currents high up in the sky, wind turbines are often over 70 metres tall. When wind flows across the blades of the wind turbine, these blades capture the kinetic energy from the wind and transform it into rotational energy. This causes them to spin. The blades are connected to the generator, either directly or through a shaft and gears. The spinning blades drive the generator, which generates electricity.

Advantages of Wind Power

Wind is a source of renewable energy, meaning that there are no fuel costs and the process does not use up finite resources. Also, the process does not produce any harmful emissions, unlike burning fossil fuels (coal, oil and natural gas), which produces carbon dioxide.

Disadvantages of Wind Power

Sourcing energy from the wind is temperamental. The amount of electricity produced depends on the strength of the wind. If there is no wind, there is no electricity.

1 How many wind turbines will there
be in the Jiuquan Wind Power Base?

....

....

2 What are the three fossil fuels mentioned in the text?

....

....

....

3 Why is renewable energy popular amongst
the environmentally conscious? Give two reasons.

....

....

....

....

4 What does grinding grain produce?

....

5 What did Professor James Blyth achieve in 1887?

....

6 What were windmills used for in the 9th century?
Circle the correct answers.

| grinding grain | generating electricity | pumping water |

7 **What type of energy do wind turbines transform kinetic energy into?**

....

8 **Why do you think wind farms are built in "flat, open areas"?**

....

....

....

9 **Create a persuasive poster to promote the benefits of wind power.**

In your poster, you will need to explain how it works and argue why you think it is a good way to generate energy. To help you write this poster, here are some writing goals:

1.   Write a headline that summarises your opinion. It might be something like, **MORE WIND TURBINES!**

2.   Write a short introduction explaining what wind power is and how it works:

     a.   Include at least one fact. Highlight the most helpful information from the article and find a way to rewrite it in your own words.

     b.   Use precise vocabulary, like **rotational energy** or **generator**.

     c.   For an extra challenge, draw a diagram in this section to help your reader understand how wind turbines work!

3.   Explain your opinion. This might be a list of reasons why you think more wind farms should be built. This section is where you really need to **persuade** the reader.

4.   Write a conclusion. In your conclusion, you might give your reader the best reason why they should agree with you. You might also include a suggestion for how they can help you share your message with even more people. It might be something like, **If you want to help, write an email to your local politician!** or **Make your own poster arguing for wind power!**

— Headline

What is wind power and how does it work?

Draw here

My opinion:

My conclusion:

First, you're going to read a **persuasive text**. Take your time and read the text slowly.

Then, use the text to help you answer the questions. If you aren't sure about an answer, go back and read the text again.

The main purpose of a **persuasive text** is to present a point of view and persuade the reader to agree.

DID YOU KNOW?

Persuade means to make someone do or believe something through reasoning or argument.

A **persuasive text** could be a letter to your headteacher asking for a longer lunch break, an article promoting recycling, a strongly worded movie review or even an advertisement.

TECHNIQUES FOR PERSUASION

Emotive language and exaggeration
Using words with strong emotions behind them can persuade the reader, for example, saying something is **impossible** is stronger than saying something is **difficult**.

Personal tone and direct address
Using words that make the reader feel directly involved (including **you** and **your** pronouns) can draw the reader in, for example, "**You** must agree that this is ridiculous!"

Rhetorical questions
Asking questions can make the reader consider your point of view, for example, "Do you think this is right?"

Anecdotes
Using short stories from real life can make your viewpoint more believable.

Repetition
Repeating key points can help reinforce your ideas! Repeating key points can help reinforce your ideas!

We will be focusing on a **letter** written by **a concerned pupil trying to persuade Mr Teacher to allow graffiti at school**.

Before you read the letter, here are some key words to help you understand the text.

adamant
adj. **impossible to persuade or unwilling to change their opinion**
Bearnice was adamant it was Tuesday, but Bogart kept insisting it was Thursday.

unjustified
adj. **wrong and undeserved**
The after-school detention was cruel and unjustified.

discourage
v. **to cause someone to feel less confident or positive about something**
Yin tried to discourage Yang from pranking their teacher.

dynamic
adj. **constantly changing or developing**
The rainforest is a dynamic environment. There's something new to discover every day.

remiss
adj. **careless or irresponsible**
It would be remiss of Plato not to ask if anyone had any allergies.

Dear Mr Teacher,

Having been a student here for three years now, I feel it is my duty to inform you of the pupils' adamant belief that graffiti should be allowed in our school. It has long been felt by myself and the entirety of the student body that the school's anti-graffiti policy is harsh and unjustified and suppresses pupils' artistic expression. Our reasons for these beliefs are as follows.

Firstly, art is one of the most popular subjects at this school and I know that you are a keen painter in your spare time, Mr Teacher. Just as you create your artwork with paint and canvas, a graffiti artist creates their artwork with paint and a wall. Painting a public space allows the artist to express themselves somewhere that will definitely be seen. Do you want to be responsible for discouraging the young artists of tomorrow by telling them they can't express themselves?

Secondly, graffiti is often bright, colourful and bold. It changes the character of the area it is found in. Imagine the hallways and lockers painted all the colours of the rainbow instead of their current, dull grey. Pupils would be excited to learn in such a dynamic and ever-changing environment. When I started to graffiti the walls of my bedroom, my homework scores improved by 25%.

Finally, if graffiti was actively encouraged, this school could become famous in the art world. We could have famous graffiti artists come to our school to give talks and create artwork. Haven't you always wanted to meet a celebrity artist? These appearances would make the school popular among both pupils and parents.

In conclusion, it would be remiss to discourage the artistic expression of pupils. I, on behalf of all students at this school, look forward to hearing your response.

Yours sincerely,

A concerned pupil

1 **What is the main purpose of this text?**
Tick your answer.

a. To describe the benefits of graffiti in schools. ◯

b. To explain why all art should only be paintings of elephants. ◯

c. To persuade Mr Teacher to allow graffiti in schools. ◯

d. To explain why graffiti is better than other art forms. ◯

2 **By what percentage did this pupil's homework scores improve after graffitiing their bedroom?**

....

3 **What two things does Mr Teacher create his artwork with?**

....

4 **What does the pupil state to be one of the most popular subjects at school?**

....

5 **What three words or phrases does the author use to describe pupils' opinions of the anti-graffiti policy?**

....

....

....

6 Find and copy out an example of **emotive language** in this letter.

....

....

7 Find and copy out an example of **personal tone** in this letter.

....

....

....

8 Find and copy out an example of a **rhetorical question** in this letter.

....

....

....

9 What is the purpose of asking **rhetorical questions** in persuasive text?

....

....

....

10 Find and copy out an example of an **anecdote** in this letter.

....

....

11 What is the effect of using the phrase **on behalf of all students at this school** in the final paragraph?

....

....

12 Do you think Mr Teacher will be persuaded by the letter? Explain your answer.

....

....

13 What three arguments do you think could be made against graffiti in schools? List your answers with reasoning below.

EXTRA CHALLENGE!

Try to use some of the persuasive techniques learnt in the introduction of this section.

....

....

....

....

....

....

....

First, you're going to read an **article** about the artist **Frida Kahlo**.
Take your time and read the article slowly.

Then, use the text to help you answer the questions.
If you aren't sure about an answer, go back and read the
article again. All the information you need is in the text.

VOCABULARY

surreal

adj. **unreal, bizarre or dream-like**

I had a surreal dream about a violin-playing strawberry.

evocative

adj. **making you imagine or remember something intensely**

The smell of suntan lotion is evocative of the summer.

obstacle

n. **a hurdle or barrier that you
have to overcome to achieve your goal**

I won't let any obstacle hold me back
from winning the gold medal.

emboldened

***adj.* given extra confidence or motivation**

The headteacher's words emboldened everyone
to try their best on sports day.

inspirational

***adj.* when something makes
you feel motivated or gives you ideas**

The inspirational speech made me want
to change the world.

vibrant

***adj.* lively, vivid or energetic**

The artist used vibrant colours to paint the
tropical rainforest.

symbolic

***adj.* when an object or image acts as a
symbol or represents something else**

The dove in the picture is symbolic of peace.

DID YOU KNOW?

The Surrealists were a group of artists and writers who made art
that was inspired by dreams and fantasies. Their work involved
putting unlikely objects together, like a lobster on a telephone!

Wordsmith Weekly
Art Journal

STRONGER AND STRONGER, AGAINST THE ODDS: FRIDA KAHLO'S STORY

"They thought I was a Surrealist but I wasn't. I never painted dreams. I paint my own reality."

The story of Frida Kahlo's career is an inspirational one. She was an artist who defied the odds by refusing to let anyone, or anything, make decisions for her. Kahlo overcame several enormous obstacles over the course of her life to become one of the most important artists of all time. Her legacy can still be felt in Mexican culture and in the minds of talented young women around the world.

Kahlo was born in a suburb of Mexico City in 1907 to a Mexican mother and a German father. At the age of six, she contracted polio and was confined to her bed for nine months. The disease damaged her right leg and foot and caused her to walk with a limp for the rest of her life. Sadly, this early experience was just the first of many times that Kahlo's life would be marked by physical pain.

In 1922, Kahlo enrolled at the competitive National Preparatory School, where she was one of only about 35 female students out of a total student body of 2,000. She began studying natural sciences in pursuit of her dreams to become a doctor. She was an extremely bright student who read widely across all subjects. Kahlo soon became a much-loved member of the school community and was known for her warm and upbeat personality and colourful, traditional clothes. Kahlo would later talk about how she chose to wear longer skirts and more traditional dresses in an attempt to hide the injuries sustained from her illness as a child.

Tragedy struck again in Kahlo's life when she was just 18. On her way back from school on the 17th of September 1925, Kahlo was in the wrong place at the wrong time as the bus she was travelling on collided with a tram. Kahlo survived miraculously, but she was seriously injured. She remained in hospital for a month and was confined to her bed for several more months at home. While it must have been a period in her life that was defined by both physical and emotional pain, Kahlo was emboldened and it was during this time that she unlocked her artistic potential.

"I paint myself because I am often alone and I am the subject I know best."

Stuck at home in bed for hours upon hours, Kahlo decided to paint. She requested that a mirror be hung above her bed and an easel suspended over her so that she might be able to paint herself – the only subject available to her.

Many of Kahlo's self-portraits feature the artist seated in the centre of the canvas, wearing traditional Mexican clothing and surrounded by vibrant flowers. The objects and imagery that she surrounds herself with in the paintings are highly symbolic, whether it's a branch of thorns around her neck to represent pain or butterflies to represent rebirth. She famously said, "I paint flowers so they will not die." Kahlo's paintings are colourful and evocative and have a dream-like quality that has led many art historians to associate her work with the Surrealist movement in art.

1 **Which sentence is the best summary of this article?**
Tick your answer.

a. Frida Kahlo liked flowers and butterflies. ◯

b. Frida Kahlo went to a school with 35 female students and 2,000 male students. ◯

c. Frida Kahlo became a great artist despite encountering many obstacles. ◯

d. Frida Kahlo was half German. ◯

2 **Why did Kahlo not think of herself as a Surrealist painter?**
Use the article's quotes from the artist to help you.

....

....

3 **What do you think the word legacy means based on this quote from the text?**

"Her legacy can still be felt in Mexican culture and in the minds of talented young women around the world."

....

....

4 **Write three things that you might be likely to see in a painting by Frida Kahlo.**

....

....

....

5 Fact or opinion?

Write an F (for fact) or an O (for opinion)
next to each of these sentences from the article.

a. The story of Frida Kahlo's career is an inspirational one.

b. Kahlo was born in a suburb of Mexico City in 1907
   to a Mexican mother and a German father.

c. She remained in hospital for a month and was confined
   to her bed for several more months at home.

d. Her legacy can still be felt in Mexican culture and in the
   minds of talented young women around the world.

6 Which of the following words would best replace the phrase **artistic potential** at the end of the fourth paragraph?

energy   creativity   fear   curiosity

7 What do you think Kahlo meant in the following quote?

"I paint flowers so they will not die." Tick your answer.

a. Painting flowers stops them from dying.

b. Painting flowers makes their beauty last forever.

c. Painting flowers can be dangerous.

8 Why do you think the title of this article is **Stronger and Stronger, Against the Odds**?

....

....

....

In this section, we're going to focus on reading comprehension skills when reading **fiction** texts. Reading comprehension is all about reading a text carefully, taking your time and understanding it.

Here, we'll be reading the Mrs Wordsmith version of an **Ancient Greek myth**.

Myths are stories that were created by ancient cultures to make the natural world less of a scary place. The Ancient Greeks created myths that were tied to their religion and they often involved gods and goddesses as main characters.

You can identify myths by the way they involve courageous heroes, magical powers and fictional creatures like a horse with wings.

Like fables and folktales, myths belong to the **oral tradition** of storytelling. This means that they were often passed on from generation to generation through the spoken word, instead of written down. The characters and the plot of each myth remained generally the same over time, but other details were added or taken away depending on the storyteller.

Before we read the Mrs Wordsmith retelling of the myth **Perseus and the Graeae** (a section of a much larger myth), let's take a look at some vocabulary to get us in the mood.

diligent

adj. hard-working and careful;
like a precise gardener
trimming a hedge

--- WORD PAIRS ---

diligent **worker**
diligent **student**
diligent **reader**

gorgon

n. a fictional creature with snakes
for hair who can turn anyone
who looks at them to stone

--- WORD PAIRS ---

hideous gorgon
terrifying gorgon
wicked gorgon

surreptitiously

adv. secretly or stealthily;
like when you lie low or move
carefully to avoid being seen

--- WORD PAIRS ---

tip-toed surreptitiously
glanced surreptitiously
smiled surreptitiously

crude

adj. rude or savage;
like a cavewoman who
picks her nose in public

WORD PAIRS

crude **cavewoman**
crude **manners**
crude **joke**

protruding

adj. sticking out or projecting;
like a stomach that would
fit in a pot

WORD PAIRS

protruding **stomach**
protruding **tooth**
protruding **cliff edge**

ear-splitting

adj. loud or piercing;
like someone playing
a flute right into your ear

WORD PAIRS

ear-splitting **music**
ear-splitting **siren**
ear-splitting **screech**

Perseus and the Graeae

By the time Perseus landed on the Island of Cisthene, he was absolutely exhausted. Hermes had gifted him with some winged sandals to get him there, but he hadn't appreciated how much energy it would take to remain upright while using them. The problem with all the lift coming from your feet is that your torso and your head are much heavier than you expect, so gravity has a way of taking over. Then before you know it, the wings of your sandals are flapping away diligently, taking you where you need to go, but you are suspended upside down from your ankles for most of the journey. It was not exactly the heroic look Perseus was striving for.

Perseus was there to find the gorgon Medusa, but he didn't have a clue where to start. When he asked some locals for directions, they said he had better visit the Graeae, also known as the Grey Sisters. It had already been a whirlwind 24 hours for Perseus. He'd accepted a quest to bring back the head of the gorgon Medusa to King Polydectes, he'd had a brief conversation with two Olympian gods and, to top it all off, he'd discovered that he was the son of Zeus, the god of the sky. After a day like that, you don't question it when you're told to visit three sisters who apparently share one eye and one tooth between them.

The Graeae were the only ones who knew of Medusa's location. If Perseus was to complete his quest and return home in glory, he needed answers. The only issue was that the Graeae were Medusa's sisters so they were unlikely to give up her whereabouts to a would-be assassin. Perseus wiped the sweat from his brow and approached the mouth of a cave. As he crept into the darkness, he heard the distinct chatter of bickering siblings.

"Okay, time's up Enyo. It's my turn with the tooth!" cried a croaky voice.

"No, it's my turn!" exclaimed a second voice.

"But you already have the eye, Deino," grumbled the first voice.

"Yes, but I need the tooth too, Pemphredo," spat Deino, the second voice.

"Mmmstllusngt," mumbled Enyo.

"What?" asked Deino.

"Mmmmmmmstllusngt!" she mumbled again.

"Don't talk with your mouth full," scolded Pemphredo. "It's very rude!"

"I said I'm still using it," said Enyo a little clearer this time.

"Well, at least give me the eye then, Deino," Pemphredo pleaded. Perseus rounded the corner surreptitiously and spotted the three siblings. They were quite something to behold even in the dim light of the cave. They had horrible, greasy grey hair that appeared to be crawling with insects. Their skin was grey and sagging in places Perseus didn't know skin could sag. Their empty eye sockets were perhaps their most disturbing feature. Deino was the only one with an actual eye, which was green and crudely pressed in place. All three had bare gums except for Enyo, whose mouth boasted one protruding, chipped tooth. Perseus hadn't expected it to be a molar, but then again, he hadn't expected to meet three siblings who shared an eye and a tooth either. Enyo was using the tooth to gnaw vigorously on a bone that looked as though it had been stripped of meat long ago. Perseus was relieved to see that it was probably not a human bone. Probably.

"Who goes there?!" demanded Enyo. "I can hear you breathing, mortal. Don't be shy! Come and join us for dinner."

"What's for dinner? Soup? Mashed potato?" laughed Perseus from the darkness.

Enyo looked confused. Deino blinked.

"Because they're soft and you don't have any tee-" began Perseus, before thinking better of it. "You know what, never mind. I'm here because I need to find Medusa and you know where she is. I intend to take her gorgon head back home to King Polydectes."

Enyo let out an ear-splitting cackle. In chorus, the sisters began to cry out accusations like, "How dare you!", "We'll never tell you!" and "You'll never find our sister!"

But then Deino had an idea. "Unless..."

"Unless what?" asked Perseus.

"Unless you have something to offer us," replied Deino.

"Yes, that information is going to cost you dearly!" added Enyo, catching on to the plan.

"Yes, yes, it will cost dearly... It will cost you an arm and a leg!" chimed Pemphredo.

The sisters continued cackling and howling, seemingly giddy at the thought of their wicked plan. In the midst of the commotion, Perseus leapt into the air, aided by his winged sandals, and plucked the tooth from Enyo and the eye from Deino.

"Well, I don't have an arm and a leg to offer you, but how about an eye and a tooth?" quipped Perseus, charmed by his own wit. Then gravity took over and he found himself flipped upside down and suspended in the air from his ankles once again. Perseus blushed a deep shade of crimson. At that moment, he was very grateful for the sisters' blindness.

"No! Please! Give them back!" begged Deino.

"Then you better start talking," smirked Perseus.

1 **Can you number these events in the order they happened in the story?**

a. The Graeae argue over whose turn it is with the tooth.

b. Perseus steals the Graeae's eye and tooth.

c. Perseus enters the Graeae's cave.

d. Perseus flies to the Island of Cisthene.

e. Perseus asks the Graeae where to find Medusa.

f. Perseus asks the locals where to find Medusa.

2 **Why do you think the author describes Perseus' journey to the Island of Cisthene as not exactly the heroic look Perseus was striving for?**

....

....

3 **What do you think the author means by the phrase whirlwind 24 hours?**

....

....

4 **Why do you think the Graeae are also known as the Grey Sisters?**

Use evidence from the text to support your answer.

....

....

5 **What are the names of the Graeae?**

....

6 **Do you think the Graeae enjoy sharing an eye and a tooth?**

Use evidence from the text to support your answer.

....

....

....

....

....

7 **Draw lines connecting each of these words from the text to the correct synonym.**

> **TIP!**
>
> If you aren't sure what a word means, go back to the text and use the context to help you work out the answer.

a. **vigorously**   **savagely**

b. **scold**   **beg**

c. **crudely**   **powerfully**

d. **plead**   **tell off**

8 Why did Perseus think the Graeae would not want to tell him where Medusa was?

....

9 The Graeae did not understand Perseus' joke about soup and mashed potato. Can you explain it?

....

....

10 In the paragraph beginning, **Well, I don't have an arm and a leg to offer you**, which sentence implies that Perseus is embarrassed to be upside down?

....

....

11 How would you describe Perseus' personality? Choose three adjectives and use evidence from the text to explain each of your choices.

Adjective: ....

Explanation: ....

....

Adjective: ....

Explanation: ....

....

Adjective: ....

Explanation: ....

....

In this section, we'll be reading a detective mystery screenplay. A **screenplay** is a kind of script that is written for film and TV. A script is a story that is written to be performed.

Scripts use **dialogue** and **stage directions** and tell the performers **how to say their lines**. The stage directions are in brackets and italicised under the character's name. Because screenplays are written for TV and film, these scripts also include information about **what the viewer will be able to see on screen**, including information about whether the scene is happening inside (INT.) or outside (EXT.) and whether it is day or night.

You will often see the phrase **CUT TO** in screenplays. This tells us that the camera angle has changed or moved to a different **scene**, **location**, **time** or **character**.

First, you're going to read the short **screenplay**. Take your time and read it carefully.

Then, use the text to help you answer the questions. If you aren't sure about an answer, go back and read the text again. All the information you need is in the text.

'Then the Lights Went Out' - A detective mystery

CAST

Oz
Bearnice
Brick
Armie
Yang

OPENING (EXT.): STREET CORNER JUST OUTSIDE OF THE CITY - NIGHT

We follow Oz as she walks down a dark street, lit only by street lamps and the stars. She stops under a street lamp, takes out a notepad and starts writing. We see her breath in the cold air. Her phone buzzes. She answers it.

OZ

Hello? Yes? Yes. Okay. I'm on my way.

CUT TO (INT.): LUXURIOUS DINING ROOM - WARM LIGHTING FROM A CHANDELIER

The dining room is grandiose and filled with expensive-looking items, including jewellery, paintings and vases. There are four plates of food on the dining table and three seated guests. Brick is tall and muscular, wearing a tuxedo. Armie is small and meek, wearing a tweed jacket and shirt. Bearnice is at the head of the table, wearing a purple cocktail dress. All three look incredibly nervous. We then see Oz in a dark corner of the room, notepad and pen in hand.

OZ

Tell me exactly what happened from the beginning.

BEARNICE
(quickly)

It suddenly went dark and we couldn't see anything, and when the lights turned back on, we-

OZ
(interrupting)

I said from the beginning.

BEARNICE

Of course, sorry. I'm just a bit shaken.

BRICK

We really didn't expect anything like this to happen, Detective.

ARMIE

Well, we did sxcpect something to happen. Just definitely not this. Bearnice was hosting a 'Mystery Dinner Party' tonight.

OZ
(taking notes)

What's that?

ARMIE

It's where we dress up, have a seven-course dinner in a fancy house and solve a fake crime that happens during the evening... like someone's necklace getting stolen or a priceless vase going missing.

BEARNICE
(wailing)

AND THEN YANG WENT MISSING!!!

ARMIE

We were in the middle of dessert when the lights went out.

BRICK

It was pitch black! We couldn't see anything!

BEARNICE

Then when the lights came back on...

OZ

Yang was gone?

The three dinner guests nod their heads sheepishly.

***

CUT TO (INT.): KITCHEN - STRONG ARTIFICIAL LIGHTING

We see a well-stocked kitchen with pots, pans and various utensils hanging from cabinets. The marble surfaces are all spotless. Bearnice, Brick, Armie and Oz stand around a kitchen counter.

BEARNICE

Where could Yang be? We've searched the entire house!

BRICK

Why can't we find her?

ARMIE

I'm really starting to worry.

OZ

It's okay. Nothing bad is going to happen as long as I'm here. There has to be a logical explanation for all of this.

BEARNICE

I should never have organised this 'Mystery Dinner Party'! I'm so sorry!

OZ

Don't be silly. Why don't you all go back to the dining room? I'll do one last check of the house and meet you back in there soon.

BEARNICE

Thank you for all your help, Oz.

ARMIE

Yes, it means a lot to have you here.

OZ

Don't mention it. I'll see you all in a moment.

CUT TO (INT.): LUXURIOUS DINING ROOM

Bearnice, Brick and Armie look around the dining room, astonished. All the expensive items, including the jewellery, paintings and vases, are gone.

BEARNICE

How did this...

ARMIE

You don't think...

BRICK

Surely not...

***

CUT TO (INT.): DRIVING CAR

Yang is driving a car down the road, heading out of town. We then see Oz sitting in the passenger seat beside her.

YANG

Did they suspect anything?

OZ
(smiling)

Not a thing.

On the back seats of the car, we see a pile of expensive items, including jewellery, paintings and vases. Yang and Oz chuckle softly as they drive off into the night.

1 In the opening scene, Oz receives a phone call. If you had only read the first two scenes of this screenplay, who would you think had called Oz in the opening scene?

2 Having read through the whole screenplay, who do you think actually called Oz in the opening scene?

3 What is providing the **warm lighting** in the dining room?

4 Write down three ways you can tell that this line was said loudly. Find the quote in the text to help you.

"AND THEN YANG WENT MISSING!!!"

5 What course were the dinner guests on when Yang went missing?

6 How would you describe the atmosphere of the scene in the kitchen? Give evidence of your answer.

....

....

....

....

7 After searching the house, Oz says, **Nothing bad is going to happen as long as I'm here.** Do you think she was telling the truth or lying? Explain your answer.

....

....

....

....

8 Having read through the whole screenplay, can you explain the real reason why Oz said the following line?

"Why don't you all go back to the dining room? I'll do one last check of the house and meet you back in there soon."

....

....

....

....

....

In this section, we are going to focus on reading comprehension skills when reading **fiction** texts.

REMEMBER!

Fiction texts are made up and come from the writer's imagination.

First, we will look at some vocabulary that will help you when you read the story.

Once you have read through these words, turn the page and read the story called **Oz and Bearnice's Adventure on the Lake**.

Finally, use the text to help you answer the questions. If you aren't sure about an answer, go back and read the text again.

VOCABULARY

contented
adj. satisfied and comfortable

cascading
adj. gushing, pouring or flowing quickly

moonlit
adj. lit up by the moon

luminescent
adj. glowing with light

mesmerise
v. to completely hold someone's attention or enchant them

speechless
adj. silent and lost for words

overcast
adj. cloudy or grey

gleeful
adj. happy or joyful

Oz and Bearnice's Adventure on the Lake

"Bearnice?" Oz poked her sleeping friend. "Bearnice!"

"Flerghmph?" Bearnice snorted, swatting away Oz's hand and trying to rearrange herself into a more comfortable position on the hard, wooden panels of the boat.

"It got dark, Bearnice. Wake up!"
Oz and Bearnice had been out on the lake all day. And what a day it had been! Just perfect. The two of them, alone, with nothing but gorgeous sky above them and crystal-clear water below them. They'd talked, they'd sung songs, they'd gone swimming, they'd played a nail-biting game of truth or dare. Eventually, after a great deal of splashing, goofing around and eating soggy cheese sandwiches, they had fallen asleep in the gentle late-afternoon sunshine.

"I can't see a thing..." sighed Bearnice, blinking as she slowly regained consciousness. She stretched out her arms, and then her legs, and then her back, and with each stretch she let out an adorable, contented squeal.

"That'll be because it's night time!" snapped Oz. "Somehow, we fell asleep."

While Bearnice had been waking up and figuring out what on Earth was going on (and remembering where on Earth she was), Oz had been pulling up the anchor and trying to figure out which direction was home. It was an overcast night so the water was only dimly moonlit. She could make out the faint shape of hills and trees in the distance, but it was impossible to see how far away they were from land. Oz took out her phone, but the battery was dead. They looked at each other. Oz shrugged.

"So, what do we do now?" asked Bearnice nervously. She hoped Oz would come up with a plan. Oz was usually the one who got them out of trouble. But instead, Oz looked out over the inky black water and said nothing. Bearnice's chin started to wobble. She wanted to go home. She felt cold and her belly was rumbling.

She tried her best to hold back her tears, but the longer the silence went on, the harder it became until she could bear it no longer and she had floods of tears cascading down her cheeks. Oz shuffled across the boat to give Bearnice a hug.

The two of them sat huddled together, listening to the sound of ripples lapping at the side of the boat for several long minutes until something caught Oz's eye. Reflected on the surface of the lake she saw a tiny, luminescent dot. She looked up and saw it hovering in the air above her. Suddenly, there were three glowing dots, and then five, then nine.

"Look!" she whispered to Bearnice, who had already started falling asleep again. Oz didn't dare speak louder in case she scared the dots away. "Bearnice, look!"

Bearnice opened one eye. "Fireflies," she whispered in amazement.

Oz and Bearnice gawped at the growing cloud of mesmerising lights floating in the air around them. They were speechless.

Every second, there were more and more fireflies. They were everywhere. It was like someone was turning on a thousand light switches. Oz felt like an astronaut floating amongst the stars. Then, the fireflies started to move in unison. They seemed to be forming some kind of shape. A whisk? A parrot? A banana?

"It's an arrow!" yelped Oz gleefully. "Pick up the oars. Let's follow!"

1 Find and copy one thing that Bearnice and Oz did during their day out on the lake before they fell asleep.

TIP!

If you aren't sure about an answer, go back to the text and look for clues to help you work it out.

....

....

....

2 Why do you think Bearnice doesn't know where she is when she first wakes up?

....

....

....

3 What do you think the phrase **regained consciousness** means?

If you aren't sure, use the information in the text to make an informed guess.

....

....

....

4 How do you think Oz is feeling when she says, **That'll be because it's night time?** Explain why you think this.

....

....

5 In the paragraph that begins, **"So, what do we do now?" asked Bearnice**, why do you think Bearnice cries?

....

....

....

6 Why didn't Oz call someone for help?

....

....

....

7 Out of Oz and Bearnice, who is more likely to come up with a plan to get them out of trouble?
Use a quote from the text to support your answer.

....

....

8 Write down what Oz was doing before Bearnice began to cry and what Oz did after.
Explain why you think Oz changed her behaviour towards Bearnice when she cried.

....

....

....

....

9 **Draw lines connecting the words from the text to the correct synonym.**

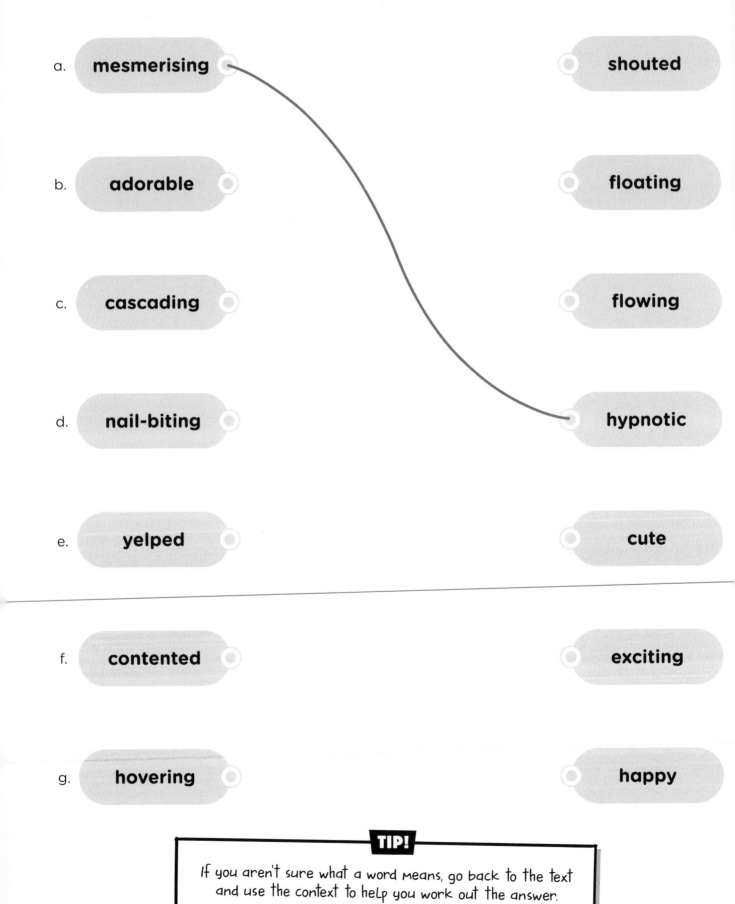

a. mesmerising   shouted

b. adorable   floating

c. cascading   flowing

d. nail-biting   hypnotic

e. yelped   cute

f. contented   exciting

g. hovering   happy

TIP!

If you aren't sure what a word means, go back to the text and use the context to help you work out the answer.

10 The author of the story uses similes to describe the fireflies. Can you find and copy one simile from the text?

REMEMBER!

A simile compares two things using the words as or like.

....

....

....

....

....

11 In your own words, describe what happens at the end of the text.

....

....

....

....

12 What do you think will happen next?

....

....

....

....

....

....

In this section, we're going to look at some writing tools that will help you make your writing fizz and pop with energy! Before we get to the tools, we need to familiarise ourselves with some key ideas:

A **literal meaning** is when a phrase stays true to its actual meaning, like **the test was easy**.

A **figurative meaning** is when a phrase means something more than the most obvious interpretation, like **the test was a piece of cake!**

Writers use **figurative language** to help them create a clear picture in the reader's mind and to make their stories more exciting. There are different kinds of figurative language, like **similes**, **hyperbole**, **metaphors** and **personification**.

A **metaphor** is a writing device that describes one thing as if it were another thing. Writers use metaphors to make writing more interesting and to help the reader imagine complex concepts easily.

The classroom was a zoo.

The classroom in this sentence was not literally a zoo. That is just the **literal** meaning.

Saying that the classroom was a zoo implies that it was chaotic and that the students were behaving like animals. This meaning is **figurative** because the combination of words in the phrase means more than just the most obvious interpretation.

1 Can you connect these phrases to make metaphors?

a. The calm lake ○ ○ is a bottomless pit.

b. Bearnice's stomach ○ ○ is an entire world.

c. The book ○ ○ is a mirror.

2 Complete these metaphors by filling in the blanks.

angel   **bird**   **little drops of heaven**   **blanket**   **exploding**

a. Hope is a little .... Don't let it fly away.

b. Thank you. You are an ....

c. The snow was a thick .... covering the city.

d. The chocolates were ....

e. My head is .... with all of this new information!

EXTRA CHALLENGE!

Describe out loud what you think these metaphors mean.

A **simile** is a writing device that compares
two things using the words **as** or **like**.

The giraffe was **as**
tall **as** a skyscraper.

The elephant's legs
were **like** tree trunks.

Writers use similes to make their descriptions more vivid
or exciting so they often include exaggeration.

① Draw lines to complete the similes!

These similes have been chopped in half. Can you put them back together?

a.   This new, luxury toilet paper is   ● ● like a log.

b.   She's sleeping   ● ● as boring as watching paint dry.

c.   His voice is   ● ● as soft as a kitten's belly.

d.   This movie is   ● ● like a nightingale's song.

2 Can you complete these similes?

This is a chance to be as creative as you like!

a. Plato was as hungry as ....

b. Have you met the wizard who is as tall as .... ?

c. Her eyes were like ....

d. The alien's skin felt like ....

3 Now it's your turn!

Can you write a simile to describe this picture?

....

....

....

Hyperbole is when people exaggerate things on purpose in order to emphasise their point.

The journey was taking forever!

Armie's bedroom is as small as a shoebox!

When people use hyperbole, they don't expect others to believe them literally because they are using figurative language.

1 **Complete these hyperbolic statements.**

Remember, when it comes to using hyperbole, you can go as extreme as you like. The more exaggeration, the better!

a. I'm so hungry that I could eat ....

....

b. It was so cold that ....

....

c. Brick is so strong that ....

....

d. Yang was so tired that ....

....

e. Bogart was so happy that ....

....

Personification is when you give an object or a thing human qualities or behaviours. It's a really fun form of figurative language!

Writers use personification to bring non-human things to life and to make their readers feel more involved in the story.

Brick could hear the doughnuts calling his name.

The flowers smiled at Bearnice as she went past.

1 **Fill in the blanks to complete the personification.**
Choose the verb that best fits each sentence.

> hugged   howled   begging   winked   refusing

a. The withered tree was .... for water.

b. The gale .... through the old house.

c. In the distance, the light from the lighthouse ....

at them.

d. My laptop is .... to turn on!

e. The cosy blanket .... me to sleep.

Writing tools like **alliteration** and **onomatopoeia** allow writers to play with the way words sound, as well as what they mean. They are a bit like magic tricks. When you use them, your reader won't always know exactly what you've done, but they'll know that something special has happened.

Alliteration is when a writer uses lots of words that start with the same sound. It is used to grab the reader's attention and to make sentences fun to say out loud. It is most often used in poetry and persuasive texts, like headlines and slogans.

Breaking News: **T**wo **t**iger **t**wins **t**umbled off a **t**rampoline.

Bearnice the **b**ear **b**lew **b**ig **b**ubbles the size of a **b**asketball!

1 Fill in the blanks with an alliterative word.

Words that create the effect of alliteration are alliterative.
Choose your own words or pick from the words below.

> pretended   salamander   greedy   purple   really
>
> gobbled   piano   snake   ridiculously

a. The .... goose .... the entire grapefruit!

b. A slimy .... slid across the sand.

c. Randy's Roller Coaster Park: .... Rapid

Roller Coasters!

d. The .... pigeon .... to play the

....

Onomatopoeia is when a writer uses a word that sounds like what it means. It can also be a word that describes a sound, like **whoosh**. Onomatopoeia is a great way to bring a text to life.

The balloon burst with a **pop**!

The bees **buzzed** around the rose bush.

① Fill in the blanks with onomatopoeia.

Choose the correct word below and use it to complete the sentence.

| bang | glug | thud | burp | sizzling | ka-boom |

a. The crying baby let out a massive .... and felt better instantly.

b. .... ! The canon exploded, sending Grit flying into the sky.

c. The door slammed with a .... !

d. Bearnice loved the sound of eggs .... in the pan.

e. Brick heard a .... from somewhere in the house and froze in fear.

f. Shang High took an enormous .... of his milkshake and left the diner.

Now it's time to apply everything you've learned so far and get writing! In this section, you will write the **introduction** to a short story based on a writing prompt.

You may remember learning about stories with four stages: **an opening, a build-up, a climax** and **a resolution**.

This is sometimes called a **story mountain** because of how the plot builds up and then comes down when a resolution is found.

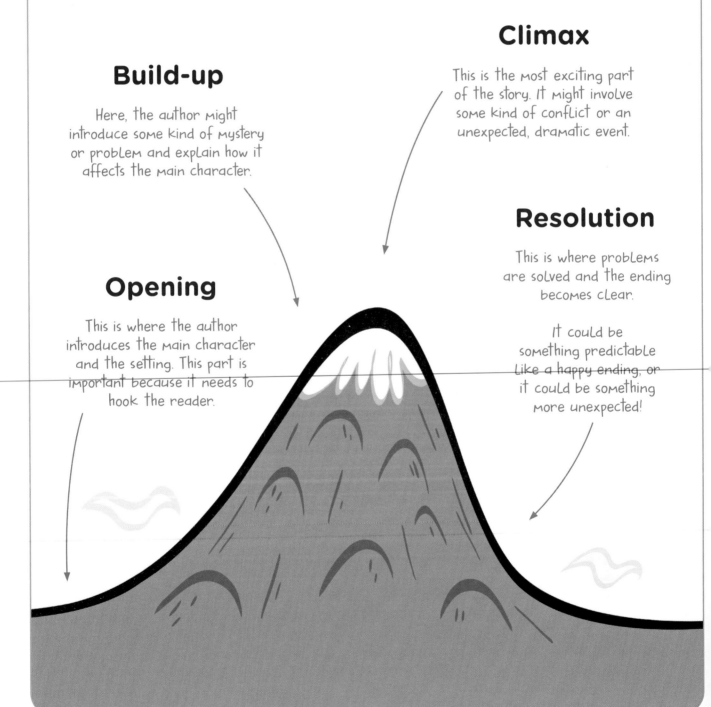

Climax

This is the most exciting part of the story. It might involve some kind of conflict or an unexpected, dramatic event.

Build-up

Here, the author might introduce some kind of mystery or problem and explain how it affects the main character.

Resolution

This is where problems are solved and the ending becomes clear.

It could be something predictable like a happy ending, or it could be something more unexpected!

Opening

This is where the author introduces the main character and the setting. This part is important because it needs to hook the reader.

Your fiction prompt is to write about
two friends setting off on a boat trip around the world.

In this task, we're going to focus on writing an **extended opening**
(this is sometimes called an **introduction**).

If enough descriptive detail is used to introduce the setting, atmosphere and characters (their appearance, personality, opinions and ambitions), then the opening can be expanded across a series of paragraphs.

PARAGRAPH 1

This paragraph should introduce the **two friends**.
Ask yourself: What do they look like? What are their personalities like?

PARAGRAPH 2

This paragraph should introduce the **main idea**. Ask yourself: Why do they want to travel around the world? What do they think the challenges will be?

PARAGRAPH 3

This paragraph should introduce the **setting**.
Ask yourself: What does the boat look like? What can they see around them?

To help you write this extended introduction, here are some **writing goals**:

Use at least three adjectives (words that describe nouns) to add descriptive detail, like **entertaining**, **arduous** or **determined**.

Use fronted adverbials to give details about the time and place, like **at the seashore** or **after sailing for four hours**.

Use dialogue, description and action to show the characters' personalities. Don't forget to use inverted commas and speech punctuation.

Use paragraphs to separate the sections of your writing.

What happens next? Where do your characters travel to? Who do they encounter?
How does the story end? Find some lined paper and try to write the build-up,
climax and resolution to your story!

WRITING

Now let's try writing a **non-fiction report!**

**Your prompt is to write a report about
an endangered species called the maganoo.**

The **maganoo** is a fictional species. In this section, we are
focusing on the style and format of non-fiction writing.
This means you will need to use formal tone, headings
and subheadings to express your thoughts and ideas.
Because the focus is on the **style** of non-fiction
writing, you can include any made-up facts you
like, no matter how unrealistic they sound!

The first paragraph is written for you, describing the habitat
of the maganoo. Your job is to then write **three paragraphs**
describing their **appearance**, **behaviour** and **diet**.

To help you write this report, here are some writing goals:

Organise the text to guide the reader using **subheadings**
and an introductory sentence to each paragraph.

Use formal vocabulary to start your sentences,
like **furthermore**, **however** and **additionally**.

Use precise language to add detail, including adjectives
like **carnivorous**, **gentle** or **nimble**.

THE MAGANOO

Habitat

The maganoo can be found in two vastly different habitats: the desert and the bottom of the ocean. The maganoo is a species native to North Africa, spending most of their time in underground tunnels. These tunnels can be up to a million miles long. The maganoo usually begin digging their tunnels near a water source, then burrow their way to the centre of a desert. Furthermore, most of their activity takes place at night as a result of the scorching heat during the day, reaching highs of 60°C. In recent years, a secondary species of maganoo known as the gilled maganoo has been discovered at the bottom of the Pacific Ocean. This subspecies burrows its way along the ocean floor, thriving in the icy cold conditions of 1°C. Additionally, there are rumours of a third species of the maganoo living on Mars, but there is no concrete evidence to support this claim yet.

Draw a picture of the maganoo to make this report more informative.
For an extra challenge, try adding helpful labels to teach the reader about the maganoo's most distinctive features.

CHEEKY CHALLENGE!

Now that you've written so much about the Maganoo, why not try to convince your friends that they are a real species? See if you can trick anyone into believing your incredible Maganoo trivia...

Now that you've written your own stories,
you're more than ready to edit someone else's!

① First, read through this text.

Shang High had believed in the existence of extraterrestrial life

(also nown as aliens for as long as he could remember. He knew we

were not alone in the univerce. He spent hours every week end

stargazing and researching unidentified flying object (UFO) sightings.

When he was younger and allowed to decorate his bedroom for the

first time, he chose bed sheets with little green aliens on and a poster

of the 1969 moon landing. He just new there was life out there.

His friends, however, was less certain.

"There's no such thing as aliens," grumbled Grit for the fourteenth time

those afternoon.

"No, come on. Think about it! Our galaxy has 300 billion stars!

Our universe has 200 billion galaxies! The universe has existed for over

10 billion years! There's so much out there. How can you think we're the

only ones.." Shang High trailed of, realising that Grit was no longer paying atention. "Are you even listening?" Shang High sihed.

"What? Yes... no. Sorry. Look, if you can show me proof like a real alien and a real spaseship, maybe I'll believe you. Until then can we talk about something else," Grit pleaded.

Shang High nods solemnly, then smiled. Grit had given his a incredible idea.

It took nine days eleven hours and forty-six minutes, but Shang High had finally perfected it. The world's first alien trap... If Grit needed proof, Shang High was going to be the one to find it.

② Now, go back and correct the errors.

All the errors in this text have been underlined and it's your job to fix them using skills that you learned in the rest of this book. The underlined mistakes include spelling, punctuation and grammar errors.

3 Can you improve this story?

You've edited to make corrections, now let's try editing to improve a text. There is hardly any detail in the description of "the world's first alien trap" in the final paragraph.

Can you rewrite this paragraph? Ask yourself the following questions:

- **What does the trap look like?**
- **How would the trap attract aliens?**
- **Is the trap successful?**

Feel free to be as creative as you like and expand your ideas across more than one sentence. Don't forget to use adjectives (words that describe nouns) and adverbs (words that describe verbs) to make your sentences more exciting.

So far in this chapter, we have done a lot of reading practice,
but really the best reading practice is reading for fun!

Here are some tips for doing your best reading
(and having a ridiculously good time while you're at it):

Create a cosy reading spot at home.
Reading time is you time and you deserve it.

Read often. Do it on the train, do it when you wake up,
do it in the bath, do it while you play basketball
(okay, maybe not that last one).

If you find yourself in a reading slump, try re-reading
your favourite book or reading the book-version
of your favourite film.

Shop around. Ask your friends and family what they read for fun.
You might be a huge fan of horror stories or books about rare species
of fish and not even know it yet. And remember, not everything you
read has to look the same.

To get inspired, let's ask the Mrs Wordsmith characters...

WHAT WAS THE LAST THING YOU LOVED READING?

Grit

I just finished reading a book called *Taking Over the World in Eighty Days*. It was really eye opening and gave me a lot to think about. There was a chapter on building an impenetrable fortress with no windows or doors so no one can stop you or your evil plans. I got a bit carried away and built one immediately. I just haven't quite worked out how to get inside yet. Aside from that little hiccup, it was an absolutely brilliant book! I didn't realise when I stole it... I mean bought it... that it's a parody of a novel called *Around the World in Eighty Days* by Jules Verne! Maybe I'll read that next to see if it has any hints about getting into your own impenetrable fortress.

Bogart

I used to lose my temper a lot. Even the tiniest thing would set me off on a raging rampage. One time, I was looking out over a serene lake, feeling totally at peace with the world, when a leaf hit the surface of the water, causing it to ripple. IT RIPPLED! The perfect view was RUINED and I hated EVERYTHING! Then I read this self-help book called *From Wagging Your Finger to Wagging Your Tail: An Anger Management Book for Dogs* and it totally changed my life.

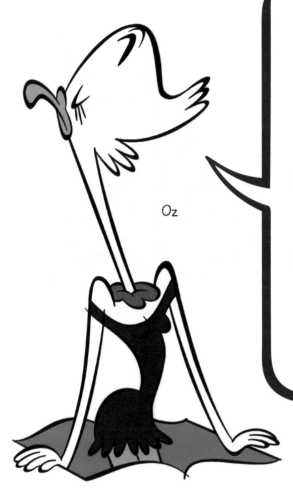

Oz

I really, really, really recommend *The Mysterious Benedict Society* by Trenton Lee Stewart. It's about four gifted children saving the world so obviously I related to them. I'm also VERY gifted. The book has so many twists and turns and puzzles to solve, you need to be quite clever to get it. I obviously got it. As well as being incredibly gifted, I'm also VERY clever. Maybe don't recommend this book to Bogart, though. The villain is trying to brainwash the world and Bogart might get ideas.

I usually only like graphic novels and comics, but *Hurricane Child* by Kacen Callender is the exception... I am obsessed! The main character, Caroline, lives on an island in the Caribbean Sea. She thinks she's cursed with bad luck because she was born during a hurricane. I think I'm cursed with bad luck because I have a twin sister who never listens.

Yin

Plato

My favourite chef is called Cuisinier Célèbre and she just released her autobiography! She's had such a varied career, from baking croissants for volunteer nurses, to stewing bouillabaisse soup for spies, to developing premium dinners for guide dogs, to making chocolate eclairs for the Swedish royal family. Name any group of people and Cuisinier has cooked for them at some point! What a chef! What a book!

Shang High

Shampoo bottles.
If you know, you know.

1 What was the last thing you loved reading?

....

....

2 Ask a few friends, "What was the last thing you loved reading?"

Write down the answer that interests you the most so you can remember to read it at some point!

....

....

Pages 10-11

1 a. abstract: danger
concrete: bees

b. abstract: fashion

c. abstract: rhythm
concrete: orchestra

d. abstract: truth, end
concrete: book

e. abstract: bravery
concrete: villagers

f. abstract: match, excitement

2 proper nouns: Venezuela, December
concrete nouns: ladybird, flag
abstract nouns: knowledge, rage,
dream, music, childhood
collective nouns: swarm, herd, flock

Pages 12-13

1 I, we, Yin and Yang, they (juggle)
she, Bearnice (juggles)

2 a. grumbles   **b.** undertakes
c. gaze   **d.** solve
e. hike   **f.** sneak
g. rambles, realises

Pages 14-15

1 a. may   **b.** can   **c.** must
d. will   **e.** ought

2 a. Armie   **b.** Shang High   **c.** Bearnice

Pages 16-18

1 Your answers might be something like:
a. irritated   **b.** furious
c. raging   **d.** resentful
e. livid   **f.** spiteful

Page 19

1 a. resentfully **b.** irritatedly **c.** spitefully

Pages 20-21

1 certain: certainly, definitely,
clearly, obviously
uncertain: maybe, potentially, perhaps,
probably, possibly

2 Your answers might be something like:
a. Bearnice **definitely** forgot...
b. Armie will **obviously** finish...
c. The hissing snake was **clearly**...
d. Certainly, Grit...

3 Your answers might be something like:
a. Yang is **potentially** planning to...
b. Shang High is **probably** taller...
c. The cowboy is **possibly** going to...
d. Forgetting your lines will
probably guarantee...

Pages 22-23

1 time: soon after that, a few
minutes earlier
place: on the space shuttle,
in the middle of the city, nearby in
the bakery
manner: almost confidently, with a
giggle, as carefully as possible

2 In the kitchen   (place)
Four hours later (time)
Very stealthily   (manner)

3 Your answers might be something like:
"Oz called everyone into the kitchen
in excitement..."
"All of a sudden, tears streamed down
her face..."

Pages 24-27

1 a. She knows 436 facts about
the ocean.
b. Yin chased **her** all afternoon.
c. Oz knew that **she** would win the
dance contest.
d. The flying pie hit **her** in the face.

2 a. Who pushed **them**?
b. They ran the marathon.
c. Please ignore **them**.
d. They fight constantly.
e. They worked together.

3 Brick and **his** treasure hunting team...
They worked together... **They** had
recently heard... nothing was going
to stop **them** from...

It was surrounded by... Brick gulped.
He approached... Nothing happened.
He fired another... Brick and **his** crew...
It didn't budge...

It was Oz. **She** didn't look happy... Brick
saw **her** face...

We are here for the treasure...
What treasure, **she** asked.

He looked up at Oz's castle... On a
nearby hill, **he** spotted... **He** realised
his mistake...

... as **he** backed away from the castle.

Pages 28–29

1 a. **When** nobody was looking, the
monkey grabbed a piece of fruit.
b. **When** the laboratory exploded,
thousands of scientists lost
their research.
c. Grit had to walk to school **until** his
bike was repaired.
d. **After** picking apples all afternoon,
Plato made a delicious apple pie.
e. Bearnice began to panic **when**
she realised she was standing
on quicksand.
f. **After** getting new braces, Oz's smile
was brighter than ever.

Pages 30–31

1 a. The bland food offended Plato, who
was only interested in bold flavours.
b. The school, which had always been
very traditional, started teaching
interpretative dance.
c. Oz turned off the music, which
nobody was listening to anyway.

d. Bearnice, who had forgotten to go
shopping, found some pizza in
the freezer.

2 **Your answers might be something like:**
a. Brick, who was only wearing a t-shirt
and shorts, stepped out into
the blizzard.
b. The book, which was 5,000 pages
long, was boring.
c. Bogart picked up the cookie, which
had grown mould in five shades
of green.
d. Bearnice stared at the painting,
which reminded her of someone.

Page 32

1 a. leaving   b. Remembering
c. getting

Page 33

1 a. After he added salt to the cupcake
mix, Grit decided to start again.
b. Being the older sister by about ten
seconds, Yin thought she was more
mature than Yang.

2 **Your answers might be something like:**
a. Bearnice climbed up into the
treehouse, which she had
built herself.
b. After watching TV all day, Brick
decided to go for a long run.
c. Bogart sent a letter to his aunt,
trying to convince her to knit him
a scarf.

Pages 34–35

1 a. The food was dropped by Brick.
b. The litter was thrown by Armie.
c. Yin was chased by Yang.
d. The flower was smelled by Oz.
e. The screen was blocked by
Plato's head.

2 a. A   b. A   c. P   d. P

Pages 36–37

1 **a.** over **b.** before **c.** to **d.** under **e.** until **f.** on **g.** until

2 **a.** on **b.** during **c.** outside **d.** underneath **e.** until

3 Bearnice travelled **to**… After trundling **over**… while sat **on** a small boulder… began to dig **under** the boulder… dug and dug **until** sunset… she knelt down **beside** her spade

Pages 40–43

1 will not – won't did not – didn't
I will – I'll who would – who'd
I am – I'm should not – shouldn't
do not – don't it is – it's
I would – I'd could have – could've

2 **a.** didn't **b.** who'd **c.** could've **d.** I'd **e.** It's **f.** shouldn't **g.** won't **h.** I'm **i.** I'll **j.** Don't

3 **I am** writing… I definitely **did not** buy… so please **do not** ask… claimed that **I would** be… **I would** like a full… and **will not** be ordering…

4 **I'm** sorry… I **shouldn't** have… I **didn't** think… think **it's** quite… I **could've** chosen… But **I'll** pretend… **Who'd** you…

Pages 44–45

1 **a.** Oz's mansion
b. Bearnice's diving equipment
c. the octopus' hat
d. the platypus' magnifying glass
e. the elves' toys
f. the chefs' kitchen

2 **a.** cabbages **b.** bunny's **c.** teacher's **d.** spies

Page 46

1 **a.** "Your toast is ready, Oz!" yelled Plato.
b. Yes, I am aware that my shoes don't match.
c. Well, I certainly wasn't expecting that.
d. No, I will never stop making my own jam.
e. "Why don't you tell me about your day, Armie?" asked Yin.
f. Tell me, Bearnice, do you have any bright pink rollerblades?
g. I am coming to the party, yes, but I still need to decide what to wear!

Page 47

1 **a.** At 3 o'clock in the morning, Plato clicked onto the next episode.
b. Twice a year, Yang visits the crystal-clear lake.
c. Sometimes, Shang High could be a little too prepared in an emergency.

Pages 48–49

1 **a.** correct
b. Bearnice lost her socks, but her feet are not cold. **or** Bearnice lost her socks but her feet are not cold.
c. correct
d. Oz wants to learn German, or she wants to learn Spanish. **or** Oz wants to learn German or she wants to learn Spanish.

2 **a.** Oz might listen to classical music, or she might listen to rock music. (also fine without a comma)
b. She dreamed of changing the world, but she just didn't know how to start. (also fine without a comma)
c. It was a very humid day, but Bearnice did not mind at all. (also fine without a comma)
d. Chess is a game for two players, but Bogart always plays alone. (also fine without a comma)

Page 50

1 **a.** Yang, a notorious prankster, snuck into the kitchen at midnight.

b. Armie, sometimes called a bookworm, reads fourteen books a week.

c. Shang High, a giraffe who loves music, knows every song ever written.

2 **a.** The bus driver, named Kai, never got lost.

b. The thief, a skilled hacker, logged into the bank system.

Page 51

1 **a.** The house is haunted by three ghosts (apparently from the 1800s).

b. Bogart (surprisingly!) didn't have a cunning plan.

2 The village (north of the mountains) was the first to be affected by climate change.

Page 52

1 **a.** Shang High — a very tall giraffe — needed special trousers for his long legs.

b. The chameleon — a colour-changing lizard — wandered through the desert.

c. Bearnice — who had never had a driving lesson in her life — sped down the motorway.

2 **a.** Plato — the hungry platypus — wandered into the kitchen.

b. A loud buzzing — similar to a vibrating phone — can be heard from the beehive.

Pages 53–55

1 **a.** "Where are we going?" asked Yin.

b. "Let go of my hair!" cried Bearnice.

c. Plato announced, "I will never cook again."

d. "I'll do my best," whispered Oz.

e. "Stop that thief!" shouted Grit.

f. Oz asked, "Can I borrow the recipe?"

2 **Your answers might be something like:**
"Where is the gym?" asked Bogart.
"I'm taking the day off," said Oz.
"I love pranks!" said Yang.
Plato asked, "Where's the nearest kitchen?"

Pages 56–57

1 ... snacks. // One... best suit." // Oz had been... to be perfect. // That night...

2 **a.** 50 of these tribes have never had contact with the outside world.

b. It spans across Brazil, Peru and many more countries.

c. This fish has teeth on the roof of its mouth and its tongue.

d. The plants take in carbon dioxide (a greenhouse gas) and release oxygen.

e. He swam for up to 10 hours a day.

Pages 58–59

1 **a.** Life Cycle **b.** Habitat **c.** Size

2 **Your answers might be something like:**

a. Snake Island

b. Uyuni Salt Flat

c. The Stone Forest

Pages 62–63

1 **a.** underwater **b.** overslept
c. overgrown **d.** overcooked
e. underground

Pages 64–65

1 **a.** deflated **b.** defrost **c.** preview
d. precooked **e.** decode

Pages 66–67

1 **a.** enraged **b.** empathised
c. encircled **d.** endangered
e. emboldened

Pages 68-69

1 **-ise:** equalise, modernise, standardise, advertise

-ate: alienate, captivate, vaccinate, motivate

-ify: simplify, solidify, intensify, diversify, notify

2 a. equalise **b.** motivate **c.** modernise
d. intensify **e.** standardise

Pages 70-71

1 Your answers might be something like:
a. something that measures heat
b. fear of snakes
c. hating people
d. using both hands

2 Your answers might be something like:
a. fake **b.** strength
c. small **d.** people

Pages 72-77

1 a. wreak, reek
b. patience, patients
c. genes, jeans
d. guessed, guest
e. led, lead
f. desert, dessert
g. steal, steel
h. aloud, allowed
i. stationary, stationery
j. heard, herd

2 a. affect **b.** effect **c.** affect
d. affect **e.** affect **f.** effect

3 a. advice **b.** advise **c.** advice
d. advice **e.** advise **f.** advice

4 a. accept **b.** except **c.** except
d. accept **e.** except **f.** accept

5 a. compliment **b.** compliment
c. complement **d.** complement
e. compliment **f.** compliment

Pages 78-79

1 a. "It's time to **hit the hay**," announced Yin as she yawned loudly.
b. "**Hold your horses**!" wheezed Oz as she struggled to catch up with Brick.
c. "I can't believe they're going to **tie the knot** while skydiving!" cried Oz.
d. Yin and Yang had to cancel their afternoon plans. No one wanted to be outdoors while it was **raining cats and dogs**.
e. Bogart will take over the world **when pigs fly**.

Page 81

1 Synonyms: gleaming, sparkling, glistening
Word pairs: water, beauty, surface
Sentence example: The thief stared longingly at the shimmering diamond.

2 Synonyms: stale, still, foul
Word pairs: swamp, pond, air
Sentence example: The stagnant river was incredibly polluted.

Page 82-83

1 Synonyms: tiring, exhausting, crushing
Word pairs: work, effort, burden
Sentence example: Moving house was backbreaking work.

2 Synonyms: slow, exhausting, difficult
Word pairs: undertaking, chore, process
Sentence example: The laborious task took all afternoon to complete.

3 Synonyms: enormous, intense, overpowering
Word pairs: pressure, urge, weight
Sentence example: Armie felt an overwhelming pressure on his shoulders.

4 Synonyms: dull, boring, dreary
Word pairs: paperwork, process, task
Sentence example: Filling in 872 forms was a very tedious task.

Page 84–85

1 Synonyms: gloomy, unhappy, sad
Word pairs: silence, mood, expression
Sentence example: Shang High had been in a glum mood ever since his favourite band split up.

2 Synonyms: miserable, inconsolable, crushed
Word pairs: expression, tears, friend
Sentence example: Plato felt heartbroken when his best friend moved out of town.

3 Synonyms: sad, gloomy, sorrowful
Word pairs: thoughts, eyes, song
Sentence example: The melancholy song made Bearnice tear up.

4 Synonyms: longing, sad, nostalgic
Word pairs: memory, sigh, tear
Sentence example: Shang High let out a wistful sigh when going through his old toys.

Page 86–87

1 Synonyms: gobble up, annihilate, destroy
Word pairs: a meal, a cake, a house
Sentence example: Brick demolished his lunch in two seconds.

2 Synonyms: eat, gobble, consume
Word pairs: a book, a sandwich, a meal
Sentence example: She devoured the whole cake including the candles.

3 Synonyms: guzzle, stuff yourself, overeat
Word pairs: greedily, hungrily, shamelessly

Sentence example: The sea monster gorged hungrily on fish.

4 Synonyms: devour, gulp, drink
Word pairs: cola, sweets, juice
Sentence example: Grit guzzled milk after accidentally biting into the spiciest pepper in the world.

Pages 90–91

1 injectsian, magision, discusion, confesscian

2 injection, magician, discussion, confession

3 a. mathematician   **b.** invention
c. electrician   **d.** extension
e. operation   **f.** confession

4 a. electrician   **b.** extension
c. operation   **d.** invention
e. confession   **f.** mathematician

Pages 92–93

1 -**ant**: inst**ant**, hesit**ant**, import**ant**, dist**ant**, relev**ant**, toler**ant**
-**ent**: innoc**ent**, pati**ent**, confid**ent**, abs**ent**, frequ**ent**, differ**ent**

2 a. distant   **b.** tolerant
c. instant   **d.** frequent

3 patient, distant, absent, important, hesitant

4 confident, innocent, different, relevant

Pages 94–95

1 a. importance   **b.** distance
c. absence   **d.** relevance
e. confidence   **f.** difference

2 a. expectancy   **b.** frequency

3 distance, confidence, differences, frequency

4 absence, importance, expectancy

Pages 96-97

1 **-able**: break**able**, depend**able**, comfort**able**, reli**able**

   -ible: horr**ible**, incred**ible**, poss**ible**

   -ably: consider**ably**, ador**ably**, toler**ably**

   -ibly: terr**ibly**, horr**ibly**, poss**ibly**, incred**ibly**

2 possible, reliable, incredible, comfortable, considerably, dependable, terribly

Pages 98-99

1 **ei**: dec**ei**t, inconc**ei**vable, perc**ei**ve, c**ei**ling

   ie: f**ie**ld, gr**ie**f, y**ie**ld, n**ie**ce

2 **a.** receipt   **b.** shield   **c.** piece

3 **a.** Auntie   **b.** receipt   **c.** shrieked
   d. relieved   **e.** hygiene

Page 100

1 **a.** their   **b.** They're   **c.** there
   d. their   **e.** they're

Page 101

1 words rhyming with "**stuff**": enough, tough, rough

   words rhyming with "**throw**": although

   words rhyming with ""**short**": bought, ought, brought

   words rhyming with "**blue**": through

   words rhyming with "**cow**": plough

2 **a.** rough   **b.** doughnut   **c.** Although
   d. ought   **e.** enough

Pages 102-103

1 **ch:** a**ch**e, **ch**orus, **ch**aracter, e**ch**o, stoma**ch**

   ph: ele**ph**ant, **ph**ysical, gra**ph**, al**ph**abet, paragra**ph**

   sc: di**sc**ipline, **sc**ene, fa**sc**inated, **sc**issors, de**sc**end

2 **a.** physical   **b.** elephant
   c. scene   **d.** descend

3 alphabet, paragraph, chorus, echo, graph, discipline, scissors

Pages 106-109

1 c

2 Intergovernmental Panel on Climate Change

3 may, c

4 **Your answer might be something like:** "The melting of ice in polar regions means that there is more water than ever in the oceans." **or** "The heating of the oceans themselves causes water to expand and take up more space."

5 **Your answer might be something like:** "Low-lying countries are closer to coastlines and other bodies of water."

6 more economically developed countries

7 **Your answer might be something like:** "The countries that are most at risk from rising sea levels are the ones that contribute the least to carbon emissions."

Pages 110-115

1 7,000

2 Coal, oil and natural gas

3 **Your answer might be something like:** "The process does not use up finite resources or produce any harmful emissions."

4 Flour

5 He invented wind turbines.

6 Grinding grain and pumping water

7 Rotational energy

8 **Your answer might be something like:** "Flat, open areas have lots of wind."

Pages 116–121

1 c

2 25%

3 Paint and canvas

4 Art

5 Harsh and unjustified and suppresses pupils' artistic expression

6 Your answer might be something like: "**adamant** belief" **or** "**harsh** and **unjustified**"

7 Your answer might be something like: "I know that **you** are a keen painter in **your** spare time" **or** "I, on behalf of all students at this school, look forward to hearing **your** response"

8 Your answer might be something like: "Haven't you always wanted to meet a celebrity artist?" **or** "Do you want to be responsible for discouraging the young artists of tomorrow by telling them they can't express themselves?"

9 Your answer might be something like: "Asking questions makes the reader consider your point of view."

10 Your answer might be something like: "When I started to graffiti the walls of my bedroom, my homework scores improved by 25%."

11 Your answer might be something like: "It makes it seem as though the whole school agrees with this pupil's point of view."

12 Your answer might be something like: "Yes, because the pupil uses so many persuasive techniques." **or** "No, because graffiti is illegal in most public spaces."

13 Your answer might be something like: "Graffiti could damage school property." **or** "Graffiti is illegal in most public spaces." **or** "Some graffiti might be ugly."

Pages 122–127

1 c

2 Your answer might be something like: "She never painted her dreams. She painted her own reality."

3 Your answer might be something like: "The impact or effect she had on the world."

4 Your answer might be something like: "Herself, traditional Mexican clothing, flowers"

5 a. O **b.** F **c.** F **d.** O

6 creativity

7 b

8 Your answer might be something like: "Frida Kahlo faced a lot of difficulties in her life, but she still managed to produce so much amazing artwork and be hugely successful."

Pages 128–137

1 a. 4 **b.** 6 **c.** 3 **d.** 1 **e.** 5 **f.** 2

2 Your answer might be something like: "Perseus flew upside down for most of the journey."

3 Your answer might be something like: "Over the past day, a lot of exciting and memorable things happened."

4 The Graeae have grey skin.

5 Enyo, Deino, Pemphredo

6 Your answer might be something like: "No, because they are constantly **bickering**."

7 a. powerfully   **b.** tell off
   c. savagely   **d.** beg

8 Your answer might be something like:
"The Graeae were Medusa's sisters."

9 Your answer might be something like:
"You don't need teeth to eat soup." **or**
"The Graeae only have one tooth so eating anything other than soup might be difficult."

10 "Perseus blushed a deep shade of crimson."

11 Your answers might be something like:
"Adjective: Brave

Explanation: He accepted a quest to bring back the head of the gorgon.

Adjective: Arrogant **or** vain

Explanation: He laughs at his own jokes and was charmed by his own wit.

Adjective: Self-conscious

Explanation: He gets embarrassed easily when things go wrong."

Pages 138–145

1 Bearnice (**or** Brick **or** Armie)

2 Yang

3 A chandelier

4 Your answer might be something like:
"The capital letters, the three exclamation marks and that Bearnice was wailing"

5 Dessert

6 Your answer might be something like:
"Tense, because everyone is asking lots of questions and they still can't find Yang."

7 Your answer might be something like:
"Lying, because in the end, she tricks them and steals a lot of expensive items."

8 Your answer might be something like:
"Oz said this because she wanted to escape the house before they realised she had stolen things."

Pages 146–155

1 Your answer might be something like:
"They sang songs." **or**
"They went swimming."

2 Your answer might be something like:
"Because it is dark" **or** "Because it got dark while she was sleeping"

3 Your answer might be something like:
"It means that she woke up."

4 Your answer might be something like:
"I think Oz feels angry because she snapped at Bearnice."

5 Your answer might be something like:
"She was cold and hungry and wanted to go home."

6 Your answer might be something like:
"Oz's phone was out of battery."

7 "Oz was usually the one who got them out of trouble."

8 Your answer might be something like:
"Before Bearnice cried, Oz said nothing. When Bearnice began to cry, Oz hugged her. She changed her behaviour because she wanted to comfort her friend."

9 a. hypnotic   **b.** cute   **c.** flowing
   d. exciting   **e.** shouted   **f.** happy
   g. floating

10 Your answer might be something like:
"Oz felt like an astronaut floating amongst the stars."

11 Your answer might be something like:
"The fireflies form the shape of an arrow that Bearnice and Oz follow."

12 Your answer might be something like:
"The fireflies help Bearnice and Oz find their way home in the dark. They celebrate their return with a cup of hot chocolate with extra marshmallows."

Pages 156–157

1 a. is a mirror.
b. is a bottomless pit.
c. is an entire world.

2 a. bird
b. angel
c. blanket
d. little drops of heaven
e. exploding

Pages 158–159

1 a. as soft as a kitten's belly.
b. like a log.
c. like a nightingale's song.
d. as boring as watching paint dry.

2 Your answers might be something like:
"Plato was as hungry as a lion."

"Have you met the wizard who is as tall as an old oak tree?"

"Her eyes were like diamonds."

"The alien's skin felt like jelly."

3 Your answer might be something like:
"The stale bread was as hard as a thousand-year-old rock."

Page 160

1 Your answers might be something like:
"I'm so hungry that I could eat every dish on the menu!"

"It was so cold that my whole body turned blue!"

"Brick is so strong that he could hold the whole world on his shoulders!"

"Yang was so tired that she slept for fourteen years!"

"Bogart was so happy that he screamed from the rooftops!

Page 161

1 a. begging   **b.** howled   **c.** winked
d. refusing   **e.** hugged

Page 162

1 a. greedy, gobbled
b. snake **or** salamander
c. Ridiculously
d. purple, pretended, piano

Page 163

1 a. burp   **b.** Ka-boom
c. thud (**or** bang)   **d.** sizzling
e. bang (**or** thud)   **f.** glug

Pages 172–175

2 nown > known
aliens for > aliens) for
univerce > universe
week end > weekend
new > knew
was > were
those > that (**or** this)
ones.. > ones...
of > off
atention > attention
sihed > sighed
spaseship > spaceship
then can > then, can
else," > else?"
nods > nodded
his > him
a > an
days eleven > days, eleven

COOKED UP BY MRS WORDSMITH'S CREATIVE TEAM

Pedagogy Lead
Eleni Savva

Writers
Tatiana Barnes
Amelia Mehra

Academic Advisor
Emma Madden

Creative Director
Lady San Pedro

Designers
Holly Jones
Jess Macadam
Evelyn Wandernoth
James Webb

Lead Designer
James Sales

Producer
Leon Welters

Artists
Brett Coulson
Phil Mamuyac
Aghnia Mardiyah
Nicolò Mereu
Daniel J Permutt

With characters by
Craig Kellman

No animals were harmed in the making of these illustrations.

Project Managers
Senior Editor Helen Murray
Senior Designer Anna Formanek
Project Editor Nicole Reynolds

Senior Production Editor Jennifer Murray
Production Editor Siu Yin Chan
Senior Production Controller Mary Slater
Publishing Director Mark Searle

First published in Great Britain in 2022 by
Dorling Kindersley Limited
A Penguin Random House Company
DK, One Embassy Gardens, 8 Viaduct Gardens,
London SW11 7BW

The authorised representative in the EEA is
Dorling Kindersley Verlag GmbH. Arnulfstr. 124,
80636 Munich, Germany.
10 9 8 7 6 5 4 3 2 1
001–328328–May/2022

A CIP catalogue record for this book
is available from the British Library.
ISBN 978-0-24155-469-2

Printed and bound in Malaysia

www.dk.com

mrswordsmith.com

For the curious

This book was made with
Forest Stewardship Council™
certified paper – one small
step in DK's commitment to
a sustainable future.

The building blocks of reading

READ TO LEARN

LEARN TO READ

Phonemic Awareness → Phonics → Fluency → Vocabulary → Reading Comprehension

Readiculous App
App Store & Google Play

Word Tag App
App Store & Google Play

OUR JOB IS TO INCREASE YOUR CHILD'S READING AGE

This book adheres to the science of reading. Our research-backed learning helps children progress through phonemic awareness, phonics, fluency, vocabulary and reading comprehension.